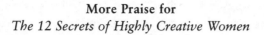

More Praise for
The 12 Secrets of Highly Creative Women

"Gail McMeekin's *The 12 Secrets of Highly Creative Women* is an unrelentless barrage of good news. It's a thundershower of inspiration, a hailstorm of possibility, a lightning bolt of vitalizing energy. Every time I sit down with it, I'm lifted up and carried away. This book is a perfect rite of passage gift for any young woman. And it's a mirror to all of us, young and old—a bright, shining reflection of what's possible when we believe in ourselves and follow our hearts. *Brava* to Gail McMeekin for this powerful and creative compilation!"

—Jan Phillips, author of *Marry Your Muse: Making a Lasting Commitment to Your Creativity,* workshop director, and cofounder of Creative Edge, a consulting firm that brings creativity to the workplace

"Gail McMeekin believes, as I do, that it is through the power of the feminine that the wasteland will be healed. One day soon, as more and more women remember who they really are—the voices and vessels of Creative Beauty—the sacred marriage of male and female energies will replenish our culture with spirit, and joy will be the offspring. Blessings to Gail for being Creativity's midwife."

—Jeanne Carbonetti, practicing artist, teacher, creative process consultant, and author of *The Tao of Watercolor, The Zen of Creative Painting,* and *The Yoga of Drawing*

"For every woman who has ever wished for an accomplished, wise mentor who would share her most valuable creative secrets, I have good news: Gail McMeekin's new book—*The 12 Secrets of Highly Creative Women*—makes that wish come true. Gail has gathered an amazing team of gutsy, smart, and innovative women who freely share their creative ups and downs, so that others may have the courage and inspiration to bring their own creative dreams to life."

—Cheryl Richardson, author of *Take Time for Your Life,* first president of International Coach Federation

"McMeekin's book puts together the pieces of the creativity puzzle in a way that explains and inspires."

—Joy Reed MacVane, M.Div., Ph.D., clinical psychologist

"Like a true synchronistic experience, Gail McMeekin's book came into my hands exactly at the moment I needed to read it. For those looking for a mentor, or for inspiration, this book is a treasure."

—Dr. Jessika Satori, entrepreneur, Venture Catalyst™, and author of *Synchronicity: The Entrepreneur's Edge*

"Our years of research and training in the creative process have taught us that nearly everyone has a far greater potential for creativity than he or she uses. This book focuses with great clarity and persuasiveness on each of the internal blocks that keeps a person from using her or his potential. *Anyone* who wants to expand her or his capacity for creative achievement can profit from reading this excellent book."

—Kathleen Logan-Prince and George M. Prince, co-authors of *Mind-Free*

"In this book, *The 12 Secrets of Highly Creative Women,* Gail McMeekin has interviewed women in a variety of creative endeavors—the arts, the media, publishing, as well as the world of commerce. What these women have in common is a sense of vision and purpose—a commitment to their unique form of creative expression that would not be silenced. A treasure trove of advice, exercises, and rich stories offers insight and practical tips. Read it, reread it, and be inspired again and again. The perfect companion for the 'creative wannabe' as she moves through her own creative process."

—Deborah L. Knox, author of *LifeWork Transitions.Com: Putting Your Spirit Online* and *Career Coach*

"I loved everything about this book—it was complete and inspiring. I especially loved the women's and Gail's stories threaded through each chapter. With generosity and empathy, Gail shares her deep understanding of the creative process with its ups *and* downs. Her book is indeed a mentor for women (and men if they choose to read it)."

—Cheryl Gilman, author of *Doing Work You Love*

"This is much more than an ordinary 'self-help book'—this book introduced me to women who are defining *success* for themselves and are willing to share their insights. I feel that I now have a whole new set of mentors who are full of heart, insight, and wit."

—Barbara G. Stanbridge, CEO, CHANGE-HRD, and president of the National Association of Women Business Owners (2000–2001)

The 12 *Secrets of*
highly creative women

The 12 Secrets of
highly creative women

a portable mentor

GAIL MCMEEKIN

CONARI PRESS

First published in 1999 by
Conari Press
Distributed by Red Wheel/Weiser, LLC
York Beach, ME
With offices at:
368 Congress Street
Boston, MA 02210
www.redwheelweiser.com

ISBN: 1-57324-141-5

Cover Design, Illustration, and Book Design: Suzanne Albertson
Cover Photography: John Freedman, Emeryville, CA
Author Photo: Gretje Ferguson

Considerable effort has been made to clear all reprint permissions necessary for this book. Each of the women interviewed for this book had the opportunity to review her quotes and biographical material. Some of the sources for the margin quotes are unknown, but every effort was made to ensure accuracy. If any required acknowledgments have been omitted, it is unintentional. If notified, the author will gladly submit those acknowledgments for further editions.

The author would like to gratefully thank the following for permission to excerpt from these works:

"Born Awake" © 1998 Clarissa Pinkola Estés, Ph.D. All rights including but not limited to performance, derivative, adaptation, musical, audio, recording, illustrative, theatrical, film, pictorial, translation, reprint, and electronic, are reserved. Used by kind permission of Dr. Estés. Poem "Anorexia Bulimia Speaks from the Grave" from *Selu: Seeking the Corn-Mother's Wisdom* by Marilou Awiakta, published by Fulcrum Publishing, Golden, Colorado, 1993. Reprinted by permission of the author and the publisher.

LIBRARY OF CONGRESS CATALOGING-IN-PUBLICATION DATA
McMeekin, Gail E.
    The 12 secrets of highly creative women : a portable mentor / © Gail E. McMeekin
      p.   cm.
    Includes bibliographical references and index.
    ISBN 1-57324-141-5
      1. Women—Psychology. 2. Creative ability—Case studies. I. Twelve secrets of highly creative women.   99-047814
HQ1206.M3696 2000
305.4—dc21

Printed in the United States of America on recycled paper.

   04 05 06   Malloy   10 9 8 7

*T*his book is dedicated with love to my two nieces, Jenna Beth McMeekin, now in her teens, and Grace Sarah McMeekin, miraculously born in 1998. My wish is that Jenna and Grace, in community with the young women of their generation, will feel empowered by this book's guidance, as well as inspired by the stories and insights of the creative women who so generously contributed their wisdom. I hope these lessons stimulate the growth of their own creative voices and spark the self-confidence they will need to follow their fascinations, wherever they may lead.

The 12 *Secrets of* highly creative women

Note to Readers

This book is designed to teach you the secrets of highly creative women. It is a guidebook meant to be read and reread over time, as you and your creative challenges change and blossom. My hope is that the wisdom of the women interviewed and the lessons you learn from the myriad of practices called *Challenges* will encourage you to soar to new creative heights and joy. This book can be your companion, accompanying you on your passage and providing you with the keys to your creative expansion.

There are three major Gateways through which you are invited to enter on this journey: Engaging Your Creativity; Mastering Your Challenges as a Creative Woman; and Actualizing Creative Results: The Power of Positive Priorities. Within each Gateway, there are a series of Secrets—essentials for a successful transition to the next Gateway. Within each Secret, there are specific Keys that unlock its mystery and spur your mastery. By the end of the book, you will have compelling goals and a plan of action steps to guide you on your chosen path. Remember, whenever the saboteur of self-doubt stalks you or you feel alone, rely on this book, infused with the many spirits of your creative sisters, to coach you onward.

I recommend that you buy yourself a notebook—a fabulous notebook, a gorgeous notebook—that you can use to record your answers to all of the *Challenges* in this book. There are twelve Secrets, one for each week or each month of the year. You set your own pace. Find other creative women with whom you can share your discoveries and struggles. Encourage each other, inspire each other, and challenge each other to bring all your visions into reality. Let's stop sparring about our differences, and celebrate our creative gifts as women. Creativity thrives on uniqueness. This book and your encounters with other women hold the spirit of a "sacred space" in which each of us can unleash our greatness.

First Gateway

Engaging Your Creativity

There cannot be too many glorious women.

—MARIANNE WILLIAMSON, SPIRITUAL LEADER AND WRITER

SECRET 1

Acknowledging Your Creative Self

Your creative self is alive and waiting for your invitation to evolve! Dare to embrace your creative self and manifest your dreams. Recognizing your creativity leads you into a life of self-expression, fulfillment, and contribution.

Keys

- Responding to Creative Callings
- Experimenting with New Processes
- Seeking Success Stories
- Learning the Secrets

> *Your creativity is waiting for you*
> *like a dancing partner.*
>
> —BARBARA SHER,
> WRITER AND CAREER CONSULTANT

*Y*es, you are a creative woman. Creativity is not just for "talented geniuses." Creativity is a tool we can all access and utilize. It doesn't matter if you've never picked up a pen or can't draw a straight line or flunked out of music class, you have a creative self waiting to be awakened or amplified. Webster's definition for the word *create* is "to cause to come into existence; bring into being; make; originate." Creative women are innovators—they manifest the new.

They dare to believe in their insights, to intuit the next step, and to take risks, even if it means getting lost or being wrong. You too can participate in creative expression and share your personal talents. You are an original; therefore, your inspirations are original as well.

As a career and creativity coach, as well as a licensed psychotherapist, human resources consultant, and trainer for the past twenty-five years, I have helped thousands of women discover and access their creative potential; achieve their personal, professional, and creative goals; and reduce the stress in their lives. It was my own personal journey, however, that deepened my fascination with the creative process and was the catalyst for my own creative awakening. That journey, which gave birth to this book, began quite unexpectedly.

When I was thirty-five and in the midst of a successful career, I was suddenly overcome by chronic fatigue syndrome. I was exhausted and plagued by a number of terrifying physical symptoms. I had all kinds of x-rays and diagnostic tests, including an MRI to rule out multiple sclerosis when I began to have trouble walking, but they all tested negative. I saw doctor after doctor, searching for answers, but because of the negative test results they all minimized my symptoms and wrote me off as possibly depressed. As a trained psychotherapist, I knew the symptoms of depression and would have gladly taken Prozac if that made

We need to remember that we are all created creative and can invent new scenarios as frequently as they are needed.
—MAYA ANGELOU,
POET AND WRITER

sense, but I was running a temperature, experiencing numbness in the left side of my body, overreacting to medications, having heart attack symptoms, and feeling too tired to perform the tasks of daily living. I was not depressed, just tired. I got up every day wanting to chase my goals, not escape from them. To me, life had always been a seductive, stunningly gorgeous, and appetizing buffet table—but suddenly I couldn't stand in line long enough to have fun sampling. I decided to take matters into my own hands and in the course of doing research, I found a book on chronic fatigue syndrome and diagnosed myself.

According to everything I could read on the subject, it was a syndrome, not a disease, so it was unacknowledged by the traditional medical community.

Worse yet, it was dubbed a women's illness and was too easily dismissed. I also learned that other autoimmune illnesses common to women, like lupus, had gone unrecognized for years until definitive tests were developed. No blood test for chronic fatigue syndrome was in sight, so it was up to me to try everything I could to get well. I located two doctors, one Eastern and one Western, who confirmed my diagnosis. I began intensive acupuncture treatments as well as herbal and vitamin therapies to boost my immune system. I spent a fortune on healers, herbs, and visualization workshops as well as other alternative therapies. Fortunately my intuition warned me to cancel my appointment with a nationally known physician who was later exposed for sexually abusing women with chronic illnesses after dosing them with the drug Ecstasy. As I tuned into my body, the potency of my intuition grew and guided me to the right choices along the way to recovery. The truth was that rest worked best. Similar to when I had had severe mononucleosis in my twenties, I started subtracting things from my life. I cut back on my consulting work, gave up relationships with people who drained my energy, dropped out of professional organizations and networks, and learned to say "No" more effectively. My focus was self-restoration.

Along with alternative treatments and lots of sleep, I married the man I had been involved with for years and transitioned my psychotherapy practice into more of a coaching business with an

> I think the creative process is not about creating something else; it's about the process itself creating who I am.
> —MAYUMI ODA,
> ARTIST AND WRITER

> My work is giving space to the creative spirit—learning to get out of its way and be in its service at the same time. We each have responsibility to express ourselves. And in this expression is the key to our healing.
> —GABRIELLE ROTH,
> DANCER AND HEALER

emphasis on career and stress issues. As one healer told me, I had been psychically absorbing all of the pain of my clients, and now there were holes in my aura. I knew intuitively that she spoke the truth and that I needed to create a limited and more selective client practice.

Responding to Creative Callings

In the midst of all of these changes, I suddenly became fascinated with art, beauty, and creative expression. I started buying new magazines like *House and Garden* (although at that time I had neither), *Country Living,* and *Architectural Digest,* and I craved visits to English country antique stores, watercolor exhibits, art galleries, and shops that featured handpainted anything. Color seduced me from everywhere.

I started wearing coral, red, and purple outfits to my office instead of dull navy and gray suits. I also found myself reading women writers exclusively.

Many years earlier in graduate school, my plan had been to have a clinical practice and then write self-help magazine articles and books. My excursions into writing had consisted of only a few published articles, but now my short-circuited fantasy of becoming a writer beckoned again. Several years earlier I had co-authored a book called *Fearless Speaking: A Work-Life Guide to Conquering Communication Anxiety.* My writing partner and I had secured a literary agent who raved about the book but encouraged us to pass up offers from two small publishers and wait for a bigtime publisher. Foolishly, we took his advice, but he never sold our book. Discouraged, my partner and I dropped the project, and then my partner, who kept the manuscript on his computer, mysteriously lost the files. Our already-written book vanished into oblivion. Despite the pain of the loss, I had to simply let it go. During my struggle with fatigue however, my mind, unlike my tired body, kept generating new ideas. While I felt some stirrings of recovery, a trip to the grocery store still felt like a backpacking expedition. I had transcended the New Age distortion that I was to blame for my illness and stopped trying to regain my old life. Every time I pushed

What you love is a sign from your higher self of what you are to do.
—SANAYA ROMAN, WRITER

myself to do work that was overly stressful just to earn money, I relapsed immediately. I finally understood. It was time to redesign my life in line with my limitations and with total allegiance to my truth.

Experimenting with New Processes

I learned about a creativity class called "Technologies for Creating" based on the work of Robert Fritz, author of *The Path of Least Resistance: Learning to Become the Creative Force in Your Own Life*. My teacher was Marilyn Veltrop, whom you will meet in this book, and who is now one of my best friends. From Marilyn, I learned about the concept of "structural tension" as a key part of the creative process. The dance between a vision of "what I wanted" and "my current reality" challenged me to engage with my creative energy and reinvent my life. I needed to stop seeing my chronic fatigue as simply a problem to be solved and instead needed to focus on manifesting my vision of a balanced, fulfilling life. The truth was that I was ready for a major work transition. Like so many other midlife women, I was burned out from too much caretaking. I yearned for a gentler, slower pace and wanted to express my creativity more directly. The nurturance of marriage and decorating a home beckoned as well. The tools I learned in class with Marilyn made the venture of reconfiguring my life all the more enticing. One of the goals I set in her class was to begin writing, immediately.

Dressed in my pajamas, I wrote the script for my audiocassette workshop called *Positive Choices: From Stress To Serenity,* based on the stress workshop I had developed and been teaching for years. My goal was to create a "portable" workshop so I could stop traveling. Creating the tape preserved my energy and reconnected me with my desire to write as a way of teaching.

Heeding my awakened intuitive attraction to art, I dared to enroll in watercolor classes with an expressive therapist and produced a collection of amateur but meaningful paintings. Pictures of lots of women locked up in stone castles revealed my dark struggle with our male-dominated society. My illness kept teaching me that

One exciting aspect of the current ferment by women is the fact that as they struggle for authenticity, they simultaneously illuminate their personal creativity.
—JEAN BAKER MILLER, WOMEN'S RESEARCHER AND WRITER

Making art is a rite of initiation. People change their souls.
—JULIA CAMERON, WRITER

subduing my feminine side was dangerous for me. I needed to stop competing in the corporate world and reconnect with my artistic, intuitive feminine self. I, like so many women of my generation, had an imbalance of masculine and feminine energies, with too much emphasis on my active, masculine aspect and not enough on my receptive, feminine energy. Playing with colors and being given permission to just paint what I felt and not worry about "how good it was" freed me to express all my creative impulses without judgment. My love of art had been slaughtered early on by a cruel art teacher, and I had been too scared to try painting again until these classes. Painting, writing, decorating, and gardening emerged as glorious expressions of my awakened creative self. My inner knowing and trust in my feminine intuitive strength continued to grow stronger and more reliable.

Some time later, I had a wonderful opportunity to study with George Prince, founder of Synectics, an innovation consulting company headquartered in Cambridge, Massachusetts, and his wife Kathleen Logan-Prince, M.S.W. Through their Mind-Free Program™, I learned about the positive power of mistakes and our self-imposed limitations on the creative process. Armed with a series of new techniques, my ability to make new connections and design novel options increased. The process also transformed my fear of being wrong. Taking risks and experimenting with possibilities became more comfortable and even fun when I let go of my terror of being criticized or fumbling foolishly. These added tools, combined with my new ability to both write and paint freely, set my cycle of rebirth in motion.

After several years on this creative adventure with more published articles, piles of watercolors, multicolored clothes, and a redecorated home, I had to acknowledge that I was indeed an artist at heart. I've always been intrigued by creative souls. Those years of running myself ragged with workaholism and denying my feminine expression had eclipsed my true spirit. I appreciated my mother's creativity, almost for the first time, and began practicing and enjoying her art, which was flower arranging. Suddenly I was drawn to attending house and garden tours and reveled in the annual "Art in Bloom" event at the Museum of Fine Arts in

Boston, at which she used to exhibit. How was it that I had never gone in to see what she had done during all those years? I suddenly felt a new freedom to choose my own feminine path. Apis, a homeopathic remedy made from bees, miraculously cooled down my fevers. Astrology readings also reassured me that I would one day be stronger. I needed that faith. Claiming my artistic self as a woman became the path to healing and recreating my life. While I still needed lots of naps and had limited energy reserves, I emerged from my transition charged with creative confidence.

Even though I was disenchanted with male-dominated corporate America, I had no interest in embracing the starving artist lifestyle. Since the Medici family was long since dead, and other patrons of the arts were scarce, what were the options for creative souls in this culture? Fortunately I had my career and creativity coaching business to sustain me. For many women, though, fears, particularly concerning money, can be a major obstacle to taking creative risks. For so many of us, breaking free of our societal and psychological chains is a prerequisite to truly creating a life that expresses our genuineness and uniqueness.

Seeking Success Stories

In my early readings on creativity, I was struck by the absence of women in the literature. Except for the regulars like Martha Graham and Georgia O'Keeffe, anthologies on creative people told stories only of men. I vividly remember being a child in elementary school and assuming creative women didn't exist, except for a few rare examples like Elizabeth Blackwell and Madame Curie. This vacuum of education about women's lives had a profound unconscious impact on me; it implied impossibility and danger. If there were no examples of creative women to fantasize about, how could we be expected to dream in that direction? While we now have women's studies programs, I have talked with many women and adolescent girls who still express the same longing to know the details of the lives of creative women that I felt thirty years ago.

As I undertook to transform my life in midstream, I began to look for the mentors of advanced creativity. Who were the best role models of successful creative women? Why this gap of information and stories about women who use their creativity to create products and services and support themselves successfully with their talent? Who succeeds and how were my questions; I wanted a thoughtful road map. I had heard from so many women over the years that self-employment or careers in the arts were "impractical." I knew that the average writer in this country makes a subsistence income and faces increasing competition. Yet, every year women publish books, design clothing, create pots, and begin businesses, and I wanted to know what separated the women who do from the women who just dream about it. Now, some women are also running multimillion-dollar businesses. Although many of these women are in partnership with their husbands or fathers or inherited the businesses, an increasing number have done it on their own. That kind of monetary achievement and level of responsibility is not everyone's definition of success, though.

Other creative women earn just enough to support their needs, choosing lifestyle and balance over income. They, too, are successful—but by their own parameters.

With this in mind, several years ago I began a journey of interviewing creative women and reading about the struggles and triumphs of others, with the intent of writing a book. My quest was to identify the skills and strategies successful creative women use to transcend the confusion of being a woman in this culture and hold steady on their creative course. I began teaching workshops for creative women and collecting information about creative catalysts. My own creative process took me in many directions during the writing of this book, but my commitment held steadfast. Giving up was simply not an option. I felt as Sarah Ban Breathnach did about *Simple Abundance,* when she told me, "This is the book I was born to write." So I carefully filed my rejection letters from agents and publishers and kept sending out my proposal. Fortunately, I was heartened by many kind and encouraging words about the project along the way. Finally, serendipity intervened and I was led to Mary Jane Ryan at Conari Press.

In the sacred traditions, the first thing you do in the morning is ask for blessings from the four elements: earth, air, fire, and water. Because all of the work that you are going to do that day will change the universe.

—LAURA ESQUIVEL, WRITER

Learning the Secrets

My interviews fueled my mission to help women recognize and express their creative powers. For years, I have seen talented, accomplished women as clients and watched them deny or downplay their abilities and achievements. For some, childbirth remains the only safe realm of female creativity. Yet we women express our creative selves with every business idea brainstormed, every garden planted, every family member or friend comforted, every outspoken word voiced, and every feminine value expressed. Sadly, the creative impulses of too many women are asleep—dormant or unacknowledged.

That's why this book is exclusively about creative women. Even in today's world of post–women's liberation, our challenges are still formidable.

We continue to be stifled by a host of factors that cause us to censor our inner voices and follow someone else's dream. That's why this book serves as a remedy. It will both affirm and jumpstart your creative power and guide you on your journey of risk and triumph. By reading the compelling vignettes of your imaginative sisters, noting their solid advice, and completing a series of practices called *Challenges,* you will be roused to spread your creative wings and ascend to new heights. As we go into the twenty-first century, the world needs the collective power of a feminine Renaissance. Perhaps that is why there are more girl babies being born this decade. Invoking the creative awareness of large numbers of women has the potential to mobilize solutions for the staggering challenges of our time, as well as helping us individually to revel in fulfilling lives.

The women who volunteered to contribute their stories here shared their secrets in the spirit of abundance—believing that we all benefit from the self-expression of others and that there is enough to go around. They offered to be mentors so you, too, can grow. Creativity is a language that crosses all cultural and economic barriers. When our female ancestors sat in sacred circles, creative tools and spiritual practices were willingly taught and passed down to young women by their elders. Just imagine how

> A playwright knows that what is most private in her heart of hearts is also the most astonishing.
> —Tina Howe, PLAYWRIGHT

many more women would have accessed their inner talents in this culture had we grown up in one of those circles of support.

Alexandra Merrill, an educator and an artist who lives in rural Maine and works with women in groups, believes collaboration is the pathway to dissolving obstacles to the expression of female authority. Invoking creative expression in ourselves and others releases tremendous power in the extended women's community.

Alexandra's work also emphasizes the value of making the most of our differences, whether they be about race, class, religion, spirituality, or economic, physical, or sexual orientation.

The women I interviewed for this "portable mentor" represent a variety of creative endeavors and have all created work I admire. To find them, I began with my own bookshelf and identified women who had served as "symbolic" mentors to me over the years. While many of the women in this book have publicized their work by writing articles and books, this is not just a book about women writers. The women profiled in the following pages represent such diverse fields as art, design, acting, ceramics, medical research, comedy, music, singing, photography, cooking, dance, psychology, and writing. Each of these women has found and expressed her creative voice as a way of finding self-fulfillment and, in several cases, fame as well.

My initial contact to these women was usually a letter explaining my vision for this book with a request for an interview. I had one cardinal rule, and that was not to chase women unless they responded that they were interested in participating. Only if they expressed an interest did I then call them to schedule a time to talk. This rule was tested numerous times. A telling example was when I received a rejection call from the assistant of a well-known artist, with the message saying that while this artist admired my project, she was much too busy with her own work to participate. I happened to mention this particular rejection to an e-mail buddy of mine who wrote back and said that she knew this artist's aunt and that she could definitely get me an interview with her. I thought it over but declined. This artist had set her boundaries and my commitment was to respect them. Boundaries are such a key lesson in this book that challenging them seemed out of line.

Be yourself.
The world worships
the original.
—JEAN COCTEAU,
WRITER

With that said, all of the women in this book volunteered their time and insights in service of your creative growth and development. It has truly been a group effort.

As a second part of the process, I told every woman that even though her interview would be taped, she would have final sign-off on her story and her quotes. All the women were thus protected by my commitment to confidentiality and accuracy, and the book includes concepts connected with specific women only with their permission. As a therapist for more than twenty-five years, there was no other way I could comfortably do this. Several of the women were shocked but most appreciative that I kept my word. Not everyone I interviewed has been included. After sorting through enormous piles of transcription pages, I selected interview material that best illustrates the important lessons, sacrifices, and conflicts about being a woman with a passion to create in this culture and at this time in history. These women have enriched my life, and my wish is that their wisdom will enrich yours as well.

The following women participated in this project, sharing their creative secrets and pathways to success:

- Marilou Awiakta: Cherokee/Appalachian poet, writer, activist, and author of *Abiding Appalachia: Where Mountain and Atom Meet; Rising Fawn and the Fire Mystery;* and *Selu: Seeking the Corn-Mother's Wisdom.*

- Barbara Baekgaard: Co-president of Vera Bradley Designs, a multimillion-dollar international company that specializes in quilted cotton luggage, handbags, accessories, tabletop settings, and women's and children's clothing.

- Sarah Ban Breathnach: Author of the bestseller *Simple Abundance: A Daybook of Comfort and Joy; The Simple Abundance Journal of Gratitude;* and *Something More: Excavating Your Authentic Self.* She is also the publisher of the new Warner Books imprint The Simple Abundance Press, as well as the president and CEO of Simple Abundance, Inc., a consulting firm, and the founder of the Simple Abundance Charitable Fund.

Creativity is like a great receptive womb.
—LYNN V. ANDREWS, WRITER

- Jan Brett: Award-winning children's book author-illustrator; her three most recent books are *The Hat, Comet's Nine Lives,* and *Armadillo Rodeo.*
- Lucia Capacchione, Ph.D., A.T.R.: Creativity workshop leader, trainer of health care professionals, and author of ten books, including *Recovery of Your Inner Child, The Creative Journal,* and *The Power of Your Other Hand.*
- Michelle Cassou: Artist and founder of the original approach to creative painting described in her book, *Life, Paint and Passion,* also cofounder of The Painting Experience Studio in San Francisco.
- Barrie Dolnick: Founder of Executive Mystic Services and author of *The Executive Mystic: Psychic Power Tools for Success; Simple Spells for Success: Ancient Practices for Creating Abundance and Prosperity;* and *Simple Spells for Love: Ancient Practices for Emotional Fulfillment.*
- C. Diane Ealy, Ph.D.: Creativity consultant, workshop leader, author of *The Woman's Book of Creativity,* and co-author of *Our Money, Ourselves: A Guide to Redesigning Your Relationship with Money.*
- Diane Ericson: Artist, teacher, coach, and designer using the company name Revisions, which features workshops and products for the art of designing; also a contributor to *Threads* magazine and co-author of design workbooks.
- Clarissa Pinkola Estés, Ph.D.: Jungian analyst, poet, scholar, cantadora (keeper of the old stories in the Latina tradition), and author of the bestseller *Women Who Run with the Wolves, The Gift of Story,* and *The Faithful Gardener.* Estés is also a social activist for the "voiceless, the helpless, and the oppressed."
- Carol Frenier: President of The Advantage Group, Inc., a marketing company in Vermont, and author of *Business and the Feminine Principle: The Untapped Resource.*
- Rosette Gault: Inventor of paper clay, international ceramics expert, and author of *Paper Clay* and *Paper Clay for Ceramic Sculptors.*

- Shakti Gawain: World consciousness teacher and workshop leader, publisher, and author of *Creative Visualization, Living in the Light,* and *Creating True Prosperity,* in addition to numerous other books, audiotapes, and videos.
- Joline Godfrey: Founder and president of Independent Means, Inc., a company devoted to the development of the economic power of girls, and the author of *Our Wildest Dreams: Women Entrepreneurs Making Money, Having Fun, Doing Good,* and *No More Frogs to Kiss: 99 Ways to Give Economic Power to Girls.*
- Janet Hagberg: Cofounder of the Silent Witness National Initiative, a domestic abuse reform organization, and author of five books, including *The Inventures: Excursions in Life and Career Renewal; Real Power;* and *Wrestling with Angels: A Spiritual Journey to Great Writing.*
- Deborah Henson-Conant: International visionary harpist and jazz musician/composer/performer.
- Loretta LaRoche: Internationally known speaker who combines stress management with humor, president of both The Humor Potential and Loretta LaRoche and Company. LaRoche also did two award-winning PBS specials, *The Joy of Stress* and *Humor Your Stress,* and is the author of *Relax, You May Only Have A Few Minutes Left.*
- Brenda Laurel: Vice president of design at Purple Moon in Mountain View, California, and a twenty-year entertainment software and technology research veteran who creates meaningful entertainment experiences for girls.
- June Levinson: Ceramist, art dealer, and jewelry designer.
- Donna Milani Luther: Creative arts teacher, Montessori principal, and national workshop leader.
- Chris Madden: Designer, owner of Chris Madden, Inc., host of her own television show *Interiors by Design* on HGTV; frequent guest on *Oprah!* and the *Today Show;* author of thirteen books, most recently *A Room Of Her Own: Women's Personal Spaces, Chris Madden's Guide To Personalizing Your Home, Bathrooms,* and *Kitchens;* weekly

columnist for Scripps-Howard News Service; and a creative consultant to Bassett Furniture Company.

- Alice Aspen March: Workshop leader, speaker, author of *The Attention Factor,* and creator of the Emmy-nominated television documentary, *Latchkey Kids.*
- Alexandra Merrill: Women's group process teacher, artist, and community organizer.
- Pam Moore: Partner and consultant at Synectics, Inc., an international consulting company specializing in innovation headquartered in Cambridge, Massachusetts.
- Patricia Miller: Co-president of Vera Bradley Designs (see Barbara Baekgaard).
- Maureen Murdock: Core faculty, Pacifica Graduate Institute, photographer, and author of *Father's Daughters: Transforming the Father-Daughter Relationship; The Heroine's Journey; The Heroine's Journey Workbook;* and *Spinning Inward: Using Guided Imagery with Children.*
- Leslie Neal: Dancer and choreographer, artistic director of Leslie Neal Dance, Associate Professor of Dance at Florida International University, and creator of "Inside Out— Expressive Arts Workshops for Incarcerated Women" at Broward Correctional Institution in Florida.
- Miriam E. Nelson, Ph.D.: Associate chief of the Human Physiology Laboratory at the Jean Mayer USDA Human Nutrition Research Center on Aging at Tufts University, assistant professor at the School of Nutrition Science and Policy, and author of *Strong Women Stay Young* and *Strong Women Stay Slim.*
- Virginia O'Brien: Career and communications coach and author of *Fast Forward MBA* and *Success on Her Own Terms: Tales of Extraordinary, Ordinary Business Women.*
- Sigrid Olsen: Owner and creative designer of Sigrid Olsen, the international fashion design firm.
- Rebecca Parris: Internationally known jazz singer, singing coach, teacher, and lecturer.

- Christina Pickles: Emmy Award-nominated actress for her role as Judy Geller in *Friends*. She recently appeared in the films *The Wedding Singer* and *Nerds in Love IV*. She is a frequent television guest star, acting teacher, and screenwriter.

- C. C. H. Pounder: Emmy Award-nominated actress who plays Dr. Angela Hicks on *ER* and has also starred in theater and films, including *Bagdad Café, Prizzi's Honor, Postcards from the Edge,* and *All that Jazz*. She is also a jewelry designer and co-owner of Banji Face Jewelry, which makes one-of-a-kind Afrocentric jewelry with a European flair, as well as cofounder of a cultural museum in Dakar, Senegal, West Africa.

- Joanne Rossman: Scarf and women's accessory designer, antique dealer, and writer.

- Cathleen Rountree: Writer and educator, visual artist and photographer, cultural mythologist and film historian, and the author of *On Women Turning 40, On Women Turning 50, On Women Turning 60, On Women Turning 70, The Heart of Marriage,* and *Cinema and Psyche: How the Movies Mirror Our Minds*. She is currently completing a Ph.D. in Mythological Studies and Psychology.

- Alison Shaw: Landscape and editorial photographer, known for her photography of Martha's Vineyard, and author of *Remembrance and Light: Images of Martha's Vineyard, Vineyard Summer,* and a children's book, *Until I Saw The Sea*.

- Barbara Sher: Career consultant and author of the best-sellers *Wishcraft, I Could Do Anything if Only I Knew What It Was, How to Live the Life You Love,* and her new book, *It's Only Too Late If You Don't Start Now*.

- Lydia Shire: Renowned chef and owner of Biba's and Pignoli's, two of Boston's finest restaurants.

- Lesley Irene Shore, Ph.D.: Licensed psychologist and author of *Healing the Feminine: Reclaiming Woman's Voice* and *Tending Inner Gardens: The Healing Art of Feminist Psychology*.

- Sidra Stone, Ph.D.: Internationally known teacher, psychotherapist, and author of *The Shadow King: The Invisible Force That Holds Women Back.* With her husband, Hal Stone, Ph.D., she co-created the Voice Dialogue technique that is described in their bestselling books *Embracing Ourselves, Embracing Each Other,* and *Embracing Your Inner Critic.*
- Marilyn Veltrop, Ph.D.: Transformational coach and guide to business leaders, as well as cofounder, with her husband, Bill Veltrop, of PathFinders, a consulting company.
- Barbara Waugh, Ph.D.: Manager of worldwide personnel, Hewlett-Packard Labs, Hewlett-Packard Company; former director of Center for Women and Religion, Graduate Theological Union; board member for State of the World Forum; associate for Global Fund for Women; and a social activist for diversity issues as well as initiator of numerous creative projects.
- Lynne Waymon: Professional speaker, networking guru, and author of *52 Ways to Reconnect, Smart Networking, No More Cold Calls,* and *How To Fireproof Your Career.*
- Carmella Yager: An artist and painter whose work has been exhibited widely and purchased for both public and private collections, she also teaches at the Museum of Fine Arts in Boston and North Shore Community College in Massachusetts, in addition to conducting private studio lessons and painting retreats.
- Marcia Yudkin, Ph.D.: Writing and marketing consultant and author of nine nonfiction books, numerous audiotapes, and an upcoming PBS series on amateur musicians.

The intent of this book has always been to share the inspirations of these remarkable creative women with you, as sisters, in a guidebook format to spark your creative unfolding. May these secrets direct you, your daughters, and nieces, and all the women of future generations toward your voice of creativity, urge you to follow where it leads, and help it flourish. The planet needs our collective feminine creative energies. Let us dare to share our knowing.

SECRET 2

Honoring Your Inspirations

In order to access your creativity, you must validate and capture your inspirations. These inspirations are precious seedlings awaiting nurturance.

- Cultivating Attractions
- Practicing Play
- Communing with Your Senses and Nature
- Taking Time to Capture Your Ideas
- Creating a Sanctuary
- Inventing Rituals

If you have a passion for something, it has an energy to it.

—JUNE LEVINSON, CERAMIST

It all begins with attraction. Creative inspirations seduce us with the power of a magnet. They lure you, charm you, tempt you, and captivate your attention. Whether it's an idea, a notion, a hunch, a whim, an impulse, a thought, an intuition, a sensation, or a feeling, an inspiration can be any stimulus that pulls you into your creative self. Like passion, creative attractions can be tantalizing. Uniquely yours, inspirations invite you into the world of creative possibility. How do you respond when an inspiration beckons? Do you accept the invitation or discount it? By honoring a personal impulse and following where it leads, creativity is born.

Cultivating Attractions

In my correspondence with cantadora, Jungian analyst, and author Dr. Clarissa Pinkola Estés, best known for her blockbuster book, *Women Who Run with the Wolves,* I asked her to describe her creative awakening. She replied, "I was born awake in this one way. In my opinion, anyone born in a creatively awakened condition deserves both congratulations and condolences." To the question, "Where do you get your ideas," she responded, "I do not have ideas. Ideas have me."

Inviting your creative inspirations into your consciousness alters the course of your life. Being willing to be creatively awake is a choice and not always an easy one. If we choose to invest in our creative self, challenges lie in wait. If we follow our inspirations, we align ourselves with our life-force and pursue a path that emanates from our very being.

Inspiration is not just the domain of the ingenious. As innovation consultant Pam Moore says, "We all have the software to be creative; we've just forgotten how to use it." By keeping our intuitive channels and our senses open to discovery, we can capture our unique inspirations. However, that's easier said than done. In the madness of this frantic workaholic era, it is far too easy to rush by the roses and never see the world around you. Too many women are overwhelmed by the awesome responsibilities of home, work, and relationships, and have lost touch with their creative voice.

In order to relate to your environment and capture your innocent thoughts or visions, you need to listen, observe, and stay centered. This capacity to linger in the unknown and see what happens is the passage to your creative self.

Practicing Play

In addition to receptivity and time, we must also grant ourselves the freedom to play creatively. Painter Michelle Cassou, founder of an original approach to creative painting described in her book, *Life, Paint, and Passion,* and cofounder of The Painting Experience Studio in San Francisco, urges aspiring creatives to "recover the capacity to invent that you had as a child." In fact, as a young Frenchwoman, Michelle searched unsuccessfully for the right art school and was even advised to give up painting. Luckily, at the age of nineteen, she discovered the Free Expression School in Paris for children ages five to fourteen and wept with delight. Forsaking traditional art school, Michelle simply painted with the children for three and a half years, basking in their freedom and lack of judgment. As a result, she unlocked her own creative potential. Today, her collection of paintings is breathtaking, and she continues to paint prolifically. When she moved to America, she opened the Painting Experience, workshops where she offers the richness of uncensored expression to all participants. Had Michelle ignored her attraction for painting and had she not surmounted the obstacles in her path, including the academics telling her to quit, she would have forsaken her true work and her inner self.

For June Levinson, bliss is getting down and dirty with her beloved clay. For years as an art dealer and more recently as owner of the Levinson Kane Gallery on Boston's famed Newbury Street, June succeeded at the business of art. She became a dealer because she wanted to collect art and didn't have enough confidence in her talent as a painter. But ultimately she couldn't hold back the artistic sense within her. After closing her gallery, she began beading,

We owe most of our great inventions and most of the achievements of genius to idleness—either enforced or voluntary.

—AGATHA CHRISTIE, MYSTERY WRITER

making necklaces and other jewelry, easily selling them to friends despite her determination to keep her art fun and not turn it into a business. She then discovered that she loved making the beads herself, which led her to the wonderland of ceramics.

June has been both a friend and a fellow explorer of creativity. She has a daring about her as well as a grounded practicality that is refreshing.

These days she is luxuriating in the opportunity to study ceramics at the Radcliffe College Ceramics Studio, meet interesting people, and express the artist within her, instead of promoting the artwork of others. Without all her previous responsibilities, June delights in being a beginner, "I have a lower standard for myself in ceramics than I did as a painter when I compared myself unfavorably to great artists like Robert Motherwell. When I made my first bowl, it was cockeyed and off center, but I was so excited. I brought it home and said to myself, 'The popcorn won't mind.' I use it all the time. I'm more forgiving of my results now. How censorious can you be about a bowl? On the other hand, I look at it and say there's all the wonder in the world in a little bowl." June's utter joy in the process has unlocked a whole new focus for her life. Like her grandchildren, with whom she takes exciting adventures, June's playful jubilation with ceramics has reconnected her with her own childlike wonder.

Challenge: PERSONAL ATTRACTIONS

Reserve for yourself at least fifteen minutes of quiet time every day to simply listen to your thoughts. Find yourself an impenetrable hideout (you can if you really want to) and relax into the silence. Allow your inspirations to flow into your awareness. Leave your internal censors at the door and accept whatever shows up. Sometimes ideas that seem silly hold great wisdom. What inspires you? What do you feel excited or passionate about? What kinds of books or magazines do you read? What kinds of people do you most like to talk with? What kinds of interests or projects are you drawn to in your leisure time? If you went back to school, what would you most like to learn about? What do you fantasize about? What are your aspirations?

What kinds of activities stimulate your creative expression? Do you long to paint, write, build, organize, sing, or play something? Select a method for capturing your images, such as writing, taping, drawing, role-playing. Save any thoughts or feelings you want to, but honor them all. Note everything and anything that comes to mind. What is your intuition urging you to explore or experience? Let this exercise be the beginning of a creative journal, idea book, or collage. You will be surprised at the wisdom in your own internal guidance. This daily date with your creative voice could change your life. Trust your process.

> Creativity is not a driving force. It happens. It creates itself and you have to be open.
> —MAYUMI ODA, ARTIST AND WRITER

Communing with Your Senses and Nature

The women profiled in this book describe an uncanny openness to the stimuli all around them. They notice the unusual and make connections. For instance, while I was on the phone with Emmy-nominated actress and jewelry designer C. C. H. Pounder, she commented, "I'm talking to you right now and three hummingbirds zoomed by the window, and it was almost like they stood there in mid-motion, posed, and said, 'Hello.' As that vision comes, I think, 'Wouldn't they be great in the back of a painting or on a piece of jewelry?' So it's just a little flash, but I'll remember it."

When I interviewed harpist, musician, composer, and singer Deborah Henson-Conant, she had been up all night composing. I asked her how she could do that, and she explained, "When I'm not in the 'all night' mode, I can't even imagine doing it. But the minute I *need* to work that way, I can suddenly do it. Sometimes I do it because I'm on a deadline, like when I wrote my first scores to debut with the Boston Pops, and the adrenaline gets me through. Other times I feel like a scientist working all night in my laboratory. At those times, it's not 'work,' it's exploration and discovery, and it's nearly impossible to stop once I catch the scent of what I'm trying to express. Composing, for me, is putting the sounds together so they have meaning, so they speak for my heart. My mind speaks to me in stories, but my heart speaks in music, and it's music that adds the dimensions of color, emotion, sensation, mood, and movement to the stories."

Deborah recalls a life-changing experience that occurred at age ten, when she first heard a piece by Claude Debussy: "It can't have been the first piece of classical music I ever listened to, but when I heard *La Mer* playing on the radio one day, I was so overwhelmed emotionally that I was really incapacitated. I remember I could not get close enough to the stereo. When my parents came home, I had actually crawled underneath it, under its little feet, and was lying there sobbing. I remember feeling like a craven animal; it was like needing drugs or something." In this moment, Deborah discovered the power of music to move her profoundly both emotionally and physically. Her life ever since has been the pursuit of this rapture.

Stress management consultant and humorist Loretta LaRoche uses strategies to create and stimulate new routines. Loretta is not just funny. Her humor teaches people to stop "awfulizing" and "catastrophizing" the unimportant things in their lives and to quit stressing themselves needlessly. As a result, she finds an endless array of material in the everyday: "I'll tell you what really gets me going. I walk a lot. I find that when I'm taking a walk, sometimes I'll burst out laughing because something will just hit me. I also get a lot of new stuff when I'm actually doing a talk, and I do what I call my 'Oprah' portion, where I ask people to tell me their stressors. And that gives me a whole new arsenal of material. I'll do a little repartee with people and feed them back what they're saying, and then we'll add to it. Because the whole idea of what I'm trying to promote is to exaggerate the very thing that disturbs you. Also, being out in nature certainly stimulates my creative bent. And then I try to be alone as much as I can. I really feel that's sacred time for me. I get up early, I sit in my chair in the morning, and have my coffee, reflecting on what stirs my creativity. And I read voraciously."

This ability to be receptive through the five senses is fueled by passion and curiosity. Writer, photographer, and stone sculptor

Maureen Murdock talks about this communication with the medium: "The way I work with photography is that I'm responding to the images I see in nature, isolating them, and then pulling out what I see. I may see a feature in a stone that you might not notice until it's printed in my photograph. So, it's always a kind of looking—maybe a way of saying it is that I am looking for the nature spirits. As a stone sculptor, too, I'm trying to find the face in the rock, or what the stone has to offer. A lot of my ideas come in dreams, but what inspires me most is looking at other people's art and nature."

The natural world is often a source of inspiration for creative women. Multitalented designer Diane Ericson describes her own alliance with the power of nature: "I've been making things since I was a tiny kid. I pretty much lived in the canyon behind my house. I feel like the best thing that happened to me in my childhood was that I got left alone—not left alone physically, but left alone to be who I was and explore what was important to me. So I really got to be in my own rhythm most of my childhood. I would sit for hours and watch this tiny plant struggling to come around the edge of a rock and make its way into the world. I feel like I learned everything I ever needed to know living in that canyon."

Nature has always been an inspiration for me too. I was lucky to grow up near an "enchanted forest" with a web of streams under the pine trees, as well as a nearby polliwog pond set among miles of rocks with caves to climb into—perfect settings for the imaginative escapades of a young girl and her neighborhood playmates. While we occasionally puffed a cigarette in one of those caves, mostly we acted out dramas. Alone, I relished the wonders of the seasons and felt connected to the Earth. I spent many joyful hours being calmed by the utter stillness and beauty of my pine forest and celebrating spring with the birth of the baby frogs. These places were essential anchors for me back then, just as painting on a deserted Nauset Beach on Cape Cod has become one more recently.

Many of the women I interviewed for this book remarked on the importance of daily walks and gardening. Fashion designer Sigrid Olsen says, "I can't separate the grounding of creativity

> Nature has been for me, for as long as I can remember, a source of solace, inspiration, adventure, and delight; a home, a teacher, a companion.
>
> —LORRAINE ANDERSON, AUTHOR

from that of the person. And what I do to stay centered is pretty much connected to the outdoors. I've gotten away from it because I've been traveling a lot, but I do a power walk outside every morning. Nature is the most grounding influence in my life. In good weather, I try to be outside as much as possible. I live in a beautiful area and I travel to lovely places. I spend a lot of time in California by the ocean and in the hills. If I lived in New York City all the time, I don't think I'd be able to be as balanced as I am."

Tranformational guide and coach Marilyn Veltrop says that being in the garden, walking in the woods, or walking on the beach profoundly influences her creative process. In her dissertation on the transformational journeys of business leaders, Marilyn says, "I had numerous instances where I would go out on a meditative walk in nature and sit with a question that I was not clear about. And I would get wonderful responses in short order."

For example, when I was pondering how many people I wanted to interview for my study, I found myself drawn intuitively to pick up this little branch on the path with eight side branches on it. Eight has always been a significant number for me, and this was further evidence that I had the right number. I also find myself out in the garden weeding and realizing that it is a metaphor for what needs to happen in my work."

This ability to sense and be receptive to our environments stokes the creative process. "You have to be sponge-like," says Carmella Yager, artist and teacher at Boston's Museum of Fine Arts, "so you cultivate a rich inner life—because you are going to transmit things through yourself with your own vision, or at least try to. Having the interior freedom to be clear about what is going through your filter takes a lot of sorting, examination, reflection, and time, time, time. It seems to me that there has to be room for puttering—time for just feeling and inhaling what comes in. And that's different than 'wasting time,' and it's important for us to recognize the difference and not be in such a hurry with our grand scheme."

Taking Time to Capture Your Ideas

If you are out of touch with your inspired self, making a date to connect opens the window. In the wise words of acclaimed writing teacher Brenda Ueland, in her 1938 book, *If You Want to Write: A Book About Art, Independence, and Spirit:* "Inspiration comes very slowly and quietly. Say that you want to write. Well, not much will come to you the first day. Perhaps nothing at all. You will sit before your typewriter or paper and look out of the window and begin to brush your hair absent-mindedly for an hour or two. Never mind. That is all right. That is as it should be, though you must sit before your typewriter just the same and know, in this dreamy time, that you are going to write, to tell something on paper, sooner or later.

"And you must also know that you are going to sit here tomorrow for a while, and the next day and so on, forever and ever."

Research is one sure way to explore your attractions in depth over time. Miriam Nelson was happiest as a child playing outside and doing a variety of sports. She got a pony when she was six years old, skied, swam, and played soccer. Her whole family was very active, but somehow she knew she wanted to be a scientist. As an adult, she merged her two loves of fitness and science by becoming a women's fitness expert. At Tufts University, her research on the benefits of strength training for women and how it slows the aging process as well as promotes health and nutrition is extraordinary. Miriam explains, "I loved science. I was fascinated with discovery and looking through microscopes. Every study that you do, you find out something different than you expected. We always go into a study with clear hypotheses, but we usually find some additional factors that are fascinating as well. I also love working with students—they're so enthusiastic and excited and their energy fires me up. Another benefit is getting to know personally the older people that participate in our studies. A lot of them have become really dear friends." This affection for her subjects reflects her strong commitment to her investigations and to the promise of longer and healthier lives for women.

> Creativity can be described as letting go of certainties.
> —GAIL SHEEHY, WRITER

Besides noticing your inspirations, you must find a way to capture them. Many creative women keep journals of their insights and ideas. Chronicling your awareness, meandering thoughts and feelings honors their value and signals to you that your creative process deserves attention. Sigrid Olsen keeps a sketchbook of her ideas, including swatches of fabric and color she collects.

"I might see something in a retail store, in a museum or a magazine, or on a person that sparks an idea and I think, that's an interesting color combination that I haven't put together before. We go to Europe four times a year to see the print and fabric shows and that's a very inspirational trip. And I might say, 'I love the idea of a black and white group followed by watery cool colors.' Then we'll do something hot and floral and then switch to something mysterious in spice tones. I'm always looking at the flow of color for all four seasons."

Renowned chef Lydia Shire, whose career was nurtured by Julia Child and who now owns two famous restaurants in Boston—Biba's and Pignoli's—still creates her own menus with partner Susan Regis. Lydia also deliberately collects her brainstorms: "What I do is read a lot of books and magazines. I do my homework, and something will jog my interest. I keep a kind of a balance in my head all the time. For instance, I'll think, we haven't had a skirt steak on Biba's menu for a long time and I'll say to myself—perhaps for the spring or summer—I don't want to do any more sirloin. Then maybe I'll feel like I want to be in Mexico, so we'll make white corn tamales to accompany the skirt steak or some kind of tomato dish. Or Susan will say, 'Let's do a capon.' And I'll say, 'And let's do it with this kind of marinade,' and she'll say she was thinking about the same thing. But we have fun—we go to her house or my house—and she brings her homework and I bring mine and we recreate the menu for each season, which is 120 new dishes every year just for Biba's. So I always say that I think what I get paid for is writing these menus."

Alice Aspen March is an authority on the effects of television viewing on the family as well as the coproducer of the Emmy-nominated documentary *Latchkey Kids*. As Alice has learned for herself, in order to develop our creativity, we have to give it our full

> Just don't give up trying to do what you really want to do. Where there is love and inspiration, I don't think you can go wrong.
> —ELLA FITZGERALD, SINGER

attention: "Time is absolutely vital to the creative process. We have to figure out how to take it and give it to ourselves. Only when we realize the kind of attention we need to be creative, do we realize the value of our time. I don't think any of us learned about this when we were growing up. I know I didn't. No one ever said to me, 'Alice, this is your time. What would you like to do with it?' I never saw this role-modeled either. So I have had to learn the process of asking for the time I need to dip into my creative well. And learning that has taken a very long time."

Creating a Sanctuary

Alone time sets the stage for creative reflection. A sanctuary offers a place to indulge our creative spirit to fuel our creative process. Following in the footsteps of Virginia Woolf, interior designer Chris Madden, a regular on *Oprah!* and *The Today Show,* wrote about the importance of personal spaces for women in a gorgeous book called *A Room of Her Own: Women's Personal Spaces.* Chris believes strongly that women need this place: "I tell women when I lecture around the country that not everybody's going to have the luxury of an entire room. Carve out a corner, if you have to, in your living room or bedroom, with a chair and a basket filled with things you love—books, pictures, tapes. If you don't create the space, you might not take the time."

In her own personal space at home, Chris has surrounded herself with meaningful treasures. She describes her creative space: "My desk is a vintage farm table that has a lot of soul and that's important to me. I also have a chaise to relax in, and there's an old statue from our garden that got split in half by a tree. I have a rotary phone, as I like the slow dial. On a tray I display black and white pictures of the men in my life: my husband, my father, and my sons—I love black and white photographs! Then there's my first sewing machine—an old Singer—which is sitting on what I call my generational quilt. The quilt is made of pieces of my mother's summer dresses that my grandmother sewed for my mother and was pieced together by my great grandmother. I love that it's about three generations. I also have a small wooden altar of photographs and the work of people who have passed on in my life, along with favorite boxes and rocks I've collected. On the wall I've hung big black and white poster-sized, almost abstract pictures, of rides in an amusement park in my hometown that I took during a blizzard—they bring me such joy!" Chris also has a Walkman for listening to her favorite tapes and sometimes lights small candles to enhance the relaxed, meditative mood of her personal space.

Challenge: BUILD YOUR SANCTUARY

Set up a creative sanctuary, even if it's only a special box for starters. Collect objects that you are attracted to, like photos, materials, fabric swatches, quotations, and books that comfort you or encourage you. As your collection grows, expand your space. As your creativity begins to take up more space in your life, the metaphor of more physical space for your things will support you. Spend time in your creative space regularly. If you don't have a space of your own, be imaginative. Barter services for space, borrow someone else's office for part of a day, or create a sanctuary in your car.

Inventing Creative Rituals

Rituals can spark our creative process. For some of us, a ritual can be a simple routine that readies us for inspiration. "I can't sit down and write or start a new project unless my closets and my life are organized," says Chris Madden. "Because I travel so much, there's always going to be a certain chaos in my life. So in order to let myself go and create, I need to have organization around me. When I come back from being away, as I did this morning, the first thing I had to do was clean out the refrigerator and bake something wonderful. I think it's about reclaiming my space."

Janet Hagberg, writer and dedicated advocate for healing domestic violence, begins her writing day at her dining room table with a fountain pen and a yellow legal pad, as she loves the beauty

Ritual is the way we carry the presence of the sacred. Ritual is the spark that must not go out.
—CHRISTINA BALDWIN,
WRITER

of the ink. When she finally gets to her computer, she is surrounded by angels, literally. Says Janet, "I have lots of angels—all different kinds of angels from different places that I've secured myself or people have given me. Some of them are hanging from the ceiling so they are floating around me while some of them are sitting on the windowsill. I've got one that has a nest with birds in her hair. I also have one that's blowing a horn and another one who has a wand in her hand. Some of them are pretty outrageous angels, because I like angels with an attitude. So I have some attitude angels up there, and they remind me that writing is more than just a technique, it's really a call to go deeper into myself so I can write with courage. My angels prompt me to remember that courage is always more rewarding than cowardice."

Writer and consultant C. Diane Ealy also has a room of her own filled with art and family heirlooms. My favorite story was about her rocking chair. Diane explains, "I have an antique rocking chair from my great aunt that's been passed among the women in my family since the early 1800s. Sometimes I just sit in the rocking chair and feel the power of the women back through the generations of my family."

Artist, writer, teacher, and chronicler of women's stories, Cathleen Rountree has built a huge altar in her living room with three levels filled by her work and objects that are meaningful to her. Growing up Catholic, she learned to love ritual: "I learned the importance of prayer in the sense of meditation, in the sense of an inner dialogue with a higher power." She also keeps flowers on her desk, reads a bit before she starts working, and goes for long walks on the beach with her companion Sienna, a Springer spaniel, to stimulate her creative ideas. She says, "It's such a fascinating thing, the creative process, because I find that it's seldom dormant. I mean, often in the shower, or virtually anywhere, I think of ideas. Just walking somewhere, I'll jot my thoughts down, as a piece of dialogue will come to me, or perhaps the opening of a chapter." She especially likes to work in the early morning "before the world comes alive." Cathleen and I have both read the book *Walking on Alligators: A Book of Meditations for Writers* by Susan Shaughnessy, to motivate us when we're procrastinating. Susan has a great quote in her book that says, "Cleaning ashes out of the fireplace becomes an entrancing job when you're doing it instead of writing."

My writing space is decorated with purple and royal blue flowers, my two favorite colors, as well as with my own paintings and gifts of feathers and crystals from friends. My wall of books heartens me as well. I also follow the advice of Sue Grafton, my favorite mystery writer, and keep a special journal for each writing project to keep track of any new ideas, such as, "I need to add a chapter on abundance." When I sit down to write or paint, if possible, I light a candle to signify that this is sacred time—priority time—and to create a boundary between these activities and my daily life. As "administrivia" is a daily seduction away from my creative endeavors, my candle supports my intentions. It helps me to resist phone calls and other "must do" distractions. I also have a sense that the fire helps to ward off any fear. Since I am an Aries, a fire sign, the flame also supports my image of myself as a warrior in the service of a better world. Like author Sarah Ban Breathnach, I also like to write in bed because it's warm and comfy.

Writer and artist Maureen Murdock describes her creative process as very kinesthetic: "My creative ritual is that I walk every morning and in the warmer weather I swim. And images will come to me when I'm moving. I also meditate first thing in the morning and there's not a day that goes by that I don't write in my journal, where I'm either working with my dreams or an idea." Maureen also finds water to be a strong element for her: "A lot of ideas come to me while I'm washing dishes or in the shower. One of the reasons that I like doing black and white photography is that the image comes out of the chemicals, so it's almost like the image coming out of the water. When working with groups, I frequently use the image of creating a pool of water—a dark pool or well— and calling forth the metaphors you need at this point in your life to teach you."

Another technique that stimulates original ideas is a ritual created by designer Diane Ericson after she lost everything she owned in a flood. She calls it the "clear the table" ritual. She explains, "Many creative people call their office a workroom but often it's really a storeroom. When you go into their workroom and their

> Nobody can be exactly like me. Sometimes I even have trouble doing it.
> —TALLULAH BANKHEAD, ACTRESS

work surface is piled with stuff with only one little corner free for something new to happen—that's really difficult as a support. So in my workshops I urge people to start designing with a clear table, beginning with a single object or a single choice. It frees people up to let new ideas come in." As Diane knows from a series of life-shattering losses in her own life, when the universe clears your table, you have to begin again and invent a new route. The flood taught her that life is ever-changing, not stagnant. Experimentation and the openness to try new configurations jump-start our awareness and growth.

Scarf designer Joanne Rossman stimulates her creativity by going on silent retreats for four or five days. Fashion designer Sigrid Olsen enjoys a daily hot soak in the tub: "I love water, so I have a bath ritual, lighting candles, aromatherapy, and everything. And that really relaxes me." Musician Deborah Henson-Conant uses a timer to help with motivation: "I put the timer on for twenty minutes and I say, 'Okay, you're not inspired, fine, but you're going to do this for twenty minutes.' And I discover usually that by the end of twenty minutes, I've found my inspiration." Carmella Yager carries a paintbrush around the house to prompt her to start painting, and to remind herself of her vocation, which is not housework or chores. Business owner and writer Carol Frenier reads what she has written that day before she goes to bed at night, and frequently gets answers or clarity in her dreams. While she is writing she also restricts her reading to books not on her topic. When she wrote *Business and the Feminine Principle,* for example, she read only novels.

All of these rituals encourage the deepening of your creative potential by anchoring it in daily life. Cathleen Rountree goes one step further when she says, "The creative process is like a lover, and you must treat it as such. You must treat it with respect, with regard, with appreciation, with love, with joy, with gratitude, with fear, with all the complexities of a relationship. And if you are able to give of yourself in the way that it requires, it really becomes a relationship." This bonding with your creative self entails acknowledgment and the honoring of its wisdom.

When I can no longer create anything, I'll be done for.
—COCO CHANEL, FASHION DESIGNER

Challenge: CREATIVE STYLE INVENTORY

Chronicle the specifics of your own creative style as it unfolds or takes a new twist. Write down ideas or compose a song or invoke another creative tradition to answer the following questions for yourself:

1. When did your creative awakening or reawakening occur?
2. What talents do you have, naturally?
3. Which elements (fire, water, wood, air) draw you toward them?
4. Where and when do you create? Where and when do you wish to create?
5. What activates your creative energy, and what drains it?
6. Do you use creative rituals? Which ones? If not, invent some.
7. Does nature influence your creativity? How?
8. What has been your greatest creative hurdle so far?
9. What time of day are you most receptive to inspiration?

Take note of your insights from these inquiries that illuminating your personal approach, and begin to redesign your life in a way that will maximize your creative potential.

SECRET 3

Following Your Fascinations

It takes courage to follow your fascinations, wherever they may lead. Yet, creativity demands that you trust and stay on the path despite obstacles. The good news is that it's possible.

Keys

- Taking Courageous Risks
- Intuiting New Pathways
- Developing Staying Power
- Heeding Your Heart

If you can put fear aside, you're unstoppable.

—JANET HAGBERG, WRITER AND ACTIVIST

I t's one thing to have an idea, but it's quite another to trust your idea and follow where it leads. Following your fascinations means taking risks and venturing out from the safe harbor to the open seas. In fact, according to Betsy Morscher and Barbara Schindler Jones, authors of *Risk-Taking for Women,* the original meaning of *risk* from the Greek is "to sail around a cliff." All of the women profiled in this book dared to pursue their inspirations into uncharted waters and have useful advice on the topic.

Taking Courageous Risks

There are two kinds of risks: impulsive risks and calculated risks. Impulsive risks unfold in the spur of the moment, unplanned. Often our intuition urges us to try something new and different. A few years ago I impulsively bought a handpainted table, which I enjoy every day. This table has also inspired me to try painting tables myself. No harm done. Often we get creative impulses to throw sand in a painting, print out a story on purple paper, or design a dress out of scarves. These spontaneous risks are part of the innovation process. Yet, sometimes impulsive risks, like being too candid with a client, teaming up with a business partner you hardly know, or taking on an acting role that doesn't suit you, can backfire. The old expression "Look before you leap" has some intelligence to it. Each of us has to learn our own balance between being carefree and careless. As women, many of us have been taught to be too cautious, too nice, and to play it too safe. That overly conservative style may inhibit the emergence of your creative self. To be truly creative, you must be willing to try and fail, and then get over it. You do, however, need to be able to determine which impulsive risks could be dangerous to your well-being, so you can make wise choices.

On the other hand, calculated risks are planned out and strategic, selected with forethought and preparation. A calculated risk might be taking a trip to Santa Barbara to see if you really want to live there. Part of the process would include a plan to check out employment/business opportunities in your line of work, meetings with a few realtors to learn about housing prices, and driving around and talking with people to learn more about the pros and cons of the city. Calculated risks propel us forward in a positive manner.

A calculated risk unlocked the potential of stress management consultant and humorist Loretta LaRoche. Divorced in her late thirties, Loretta followed her inner attraction for exercise and dance in her personal post-divorce quest to "go from dumpy to divine."

A single mother with three children, her first job was at a fitness center that hired her to teach people how to put exercise to music, which they thought was extremely cutting-edge. She hung on for a year but couldn't handle the meetings, sexism, and politicking of it all. So she took a risk: "I decided to send some invitations to people I knew to join me in an exercise/dance class at a local Elks Hall. And the only way I could afford to do it was to use a monthly support check from my ex-husband to rent the hall and just pray on bended knee that someone would pay and show up. Seventy-five women came. That was the beginning of my entrepreneurial career."

Loretta's story is a good example of a planned risk—she didn't hawk everything she owned, she used a specific amount of money. As her business grew, Loretta went on to score investors, open her own fitness center, and add stress and wellness classes to the mix. A nurse colleague of hers encouraged her to risk further and do a daylong stress program using humor. Loretta said to her, "You've got to be crazy—a whole day? What the heck am I going to do? Yeah—I'm funny, but this is a whole other thing." Loretta always had the gift of humor, but her friend encouraged her to blend humor and its healing properties. So Loretta created what she called "a day in a kindergarten class," complete with coloring, musical chairs, and research on humor. People kept calling and asking for more.

> And the trouble is, if you don't risk anything, you risk even more.
> —ERICA JONG, WRITER

As she worked with the combination, Loretta realized that stressed people often distort reality, and her humor highlights these distortions. By valuing her observations, Loretta developed a unique approach of teaching her audiences cognitive restructuring—how to change our negative thinking habits. Laughter is a great teacher in Loretta's hands, and her down-home views reflect back to us our overreactions to day-to-day inconveniences or irritations. Her mission now is to "abolish global whining." She works with the faculty of the esteemed Mind-Body Clinic at Deaconess/Beth Israel Hospital in Boston, speaks to packed audiences, has award-winning videos on PBS, and just published a new book.

I have to thank my husband for discovering her. A PBS devotee who usually watches science programs that are too technical for me, he came upon Loretta while channel-surfing and insisted that I watch her show, *The Joy of Stress,* since I've also spent years training people in stress management. I found Loretta captivating and refreshing and knew she was destined to be a blockbuster. My husband and I have listened to her routines repeatedly, and each time we discover a new nuance. Daring to take risk led Loretta to the creation of a new methodology for reducing stress.

Sometimes new enticements take us by surprise. Dancer Leslie Neal happened to hear about another choreographer who was working with women in prisons in Seattle. Shortly after hearing the story, Leslie woke up one morning with a jolt and a commitment to try it herself: "It's been like a calling. Whenever I begin to struggle, more opportunities come. I've found what I believe I am truly supposed to be doing, and I'm very grateful." Within six months of this revelation, Leslie initiated "Inside Out—Expressive Arts Workshops for Incarcerated Women" at the Broward Correctional Institution in Florida, which is now the longest ongoing prison arts program in the state and has received national attention for its success. Since 1994, it has been implemented in two other facilities in Florida, and Leslie has taught workshops at women's prisons in Michigan and California.

The purpose of "Inside Out" is to utilize art-making and creative expression as tools to enhance women's self-esteem and confidence, to expand communication skills and self-expression, and to encourage personal change.

With research support, Leslie is now working to develop a curriculum guide for other prison arts programs. As she writes about her work in her article, "Miles from Nowhere, Teaching Dance in Prison" in *High Performance,* Leslie says, "Why do I go to prison once a week? I go because I feel safer there, with them, than I do outside. I go because now they expect me to come. I go because I believe in the change that we have all experienced with each other. I go because I miss them. I go because they heal me. I go because I am a woman, and in them I see parts of me."

I met Leslie at a Common Boundary conference on creativity. Recently she took another risk and moved her home away from her warehouse dance studio and into a cedar cabin on an acre and a half of land so she could honor her need to connect with the peacefulness of the country: "In my studio in Miami, I created everything I had ever dreamed of having. It's been hard to move from that physical place because it represents many aspects of my driven, emerging artist over the past ten years. But now, as I move into my forties, I want to live in a place where I can feel the ground underneath me, see the stars at night, watch the cycles of the moon, and just be present in that. My inner voice is telling me to seek out those things that nurture me and feed me both spiritually and creatively." Leslie's courage to experiment, nudged by her strong intuitive sense of what's right for her, has made all the difference in her life.

Impulsive or planned risks can be either positive or negative. Negative risk taking can be reckless, dangerous, harmful to yourself and others, and even fatal.

Investing your life savings into a business that doesn't feel intuitively right to you or skipping your pap smear for two years are examples of negative risks. Positive risks involve challenging yourself, following your creative hunches, and testing your strengths. Positive risks include going back to school to pursue a subject you love, going to Paris because you feel called there, or taking voice lessons. Positive risk takers support themselves with a plan of action, even if the plan is to just experiment with an idea or a strategy.

> As for me, prizes mean nothing. My prize is my work.
> —KATHARINE HEPBURN, ACTRESS

> Solitude, says the moon shell. Every person, especially every woman, should be alone sometime during the year, some part of each week, and each day.
> —ANNE MORROW LINDBERGH, WRITER

Stepping out of the boundaries of security and stretching to induce growth are essential to positive risking. While we may be fortunate to have a strong support system, positive risk taking is a solo trip. It is an individual process of honoring your own belief system, pursuing a trail of clues, and dedicating yourself wholeheartedly to a path. The women in this chapter all took calculated risks based on the confidence that they were choosing the right course of action, even though there were no guarantees. They were curious, compelled, or challenged, but they also chose carefully to take a risk on behalf of their growth. In general, creative women don't worship the god of security; rather they respond to their inner urges to try out new inklings.

Challenge: YOUR RISK-TAKING HISTORY

What is your personal history as a risk taker? Do you take calculated risks—where you planned out the steps, or impulsive risks—with no forethought or preparation? Identify the key elements of your successes and failures with both kinds of risks. Then write down a risk profile for yourself with guidelines for future risk taking based on your past experience and natural abilities.

Intuiting New Pathways

The story of Rosette Gault, the inventor and developer of paper clay, illustrates how important following intuitive hunches is in cultivating creativity. After many years of running a successful ceramic design studio, and having become a specialist in the art of making eggshell-thin porcelain sculpture, Rosette acknowledged that she needed to invigorate her creative process.

Rosette applied for and received a grant from the Banff Center for the Arts in Canada and set out on a self-declared sabbatical. Twenty years earlier, while in graduate school, Rosette had questioned her teachers about the fragility of clay and why once the clay form cracks, you can't repair it. She was told, logically enough, that "clay shrinks," but she still wondered what material might prevent these stress fractures. Experts told her that some high-tech material would have to be developed to stop the shrinking, and if it ever was invented, it would cost a fortune to use and wouldn't be practical for use in ceramics. But Rosette stayed loyal to her dream of finding an easy answer, explaining, "The puzzle had been bugging me in the back of my mind for all those years."

While at Banff, she and another artist, a papermaker, fired clay and recycled paper together, and noted its lightness after firing. Intrigued, Rosette experimented further, trying different combinations. One day, she says, "I mixed up a batch of old brochures into pulp and put it into the clay and made a giant piece much larger than I normally would to test my limit. The form proceeded to crack while it dried. I came back to the dried-out work a couple of days later and looked at the crack and said, 'Oh yuck.' So I thought, it'll probably crack again but I'll just smear some of my paper clay emulsion mixture right into the crack, so I did.

"What did I have to lose since I had already lost the piece? I thought, well, if it behaves like normal, which I expected it to do, I figured it would crack again as it dried. Then I forgot all about it and a few days later I came back, but to my surprise, the crack was gone. The piece was dry and whole."

Not quite believing what had happened, Rosette kept quietly testing her mixture, and was fortunate enough to extend her stay at Banff to continue her analysis. Her new blend kept on working. After checking professional journals and trying her combination in different climates, she began to realize that she had indeed invented a new form of clay. Her invention (which recently was awarded a United States patent) has transformed ceramics forever. Her early puzzlement about why clay cracks emerged again mid-career to nudge her to transform the laws of ceramic history.

Another innovator, Joline Godfrey, founded Independent Means, Inc., and the nonprofit group An Income of Her Own. Both organizations are doing breakthrough work in teaching girls the values and skills of financial independence as they grow up. Joline's hope is that this next generation of girls will become more economically responsible for themselves than previous generations

> Life is either a daring adventure or nothing.
> —HELEN KELLER, ACTIVIST

of women have been. One of their programs is called Camp $tart-up™, a summer program that teaches teenage girls how to run their own businesses.

I asked Joline how she came upon this incredible idea. "I had written my first book, *Our Wildest Dreams: Women Entrepreneurs Making Money, Having Fun, Doing Good,* she recalls, "and by the time I got to the last chapter, my head said, 'This is crazy. . . . Here I've spent all this time listening to and writing about women, and if we continue to focus on women, we're doing remedial work.' The action has got to be with girls so that in ten years I'm not writing another book on issues women face because nobody talked to them when they were fourteen." Independent Means, Inc., now has ten full-time employees plus camp staff. They have reached over 50,000 girls, so Joline's vision is paying off. Like Rosette, she paid attention to her awareness that there was the potential for things to be better. Both of them created processes designed to prevent problems, whether it be cracking clay or female poverty.

Like me, Joline has a master's degree from the Boston University School of Social Work. All through her career, Joline's choices have reflected the social worker's commitment to social change. She was one of the first corporate social workers in the field, when she worked for Polaroid Corporation, and was continually asked to speak about her experiences in this new frontier. Committed to the potential for change in the workplace, she inspired many to follow her lead. Joline is such a savvy networker and collaborator that when she was ready to move on from Polaroid, she convinced them to fund her training company.

The idea for her first book, *Our Wildest Dreams,* came about after she wrote a letter to *Inc.* magazine in April 1989, blasting them for ignoring women entrepreneurs despite their numbers, and ended up being invited to lunch with George Gendron, editor-in-chief. There, she proposed the project of compiling a database of successful women entrepreneurs across the country and creating roundtable dinners to make these enterprising women more visible. The conversations among women at these *Inc.* dinners became the catalyst for *Our Wildest Dreams.* Just as Rosette dared to defy the laws of ceramics, Joline challenged *Inc.* to acknowledge the accomplishments of businesswomen.

When I asked Joline where she got the courage to continually try new challenges, she replied, "I'm not sure that I ever felt that it was a matter of courage, so much as it was a matter of survival.

"For the last twenty years, I have watched when I have begun to bounce off walls, and that's real information that things are not great. Rather than put up with a really dysfunctional, unhappy life, I have at least been able to say, 'Uh-oh, things aren't right here, and I need to find something that will make me sane and more at peace with myself.' So I've never seen my choices as being so much about taking risks as honoring what will keep me a healthy human being. I suppose that's just listening to one's inner voice in a way that, for me truly, is about survival more than courage. Many times when I have made choices and decisions, I'm scared silly. And yet I'm able to move forward or make changes because the alternative is too painful."

Artistic risks invoke new dimensions of your self-expression. Harpist and musician Deborah Henson-Conant's premiere one-woman show *Altered Ego,* a tour through her own life and imagination, is such a stretch. I first learned about Deborah's work from Eli Newberger, well-known pediatrician, child advocate, and tuba player for the Black Eagle Jazz Band. On a rainy night after a fabulous Jazz Boat Cruise with the band, I asked Eli to recommend female musicians for my book. Deborah was one, and jazz singer Rebecca Parris the other. Called "A Wild Woman" by Doc Severinsen, Deborah is internationally known for mixing story and song. But, by the early 1990s, Deborah felt frustrated with the musical constraints of traditional jazz, the physical constraints of the harp, and the whole music business. She sought out mime and theater coach Tony Montanaro in Maine and began intensive study to develop her performance skills and create a new type of performance art.

Her show *Altered Ego* opened in Boston in June 1998. Dressed in a little girl's black dress and cowboy boots, with colored ribbons braided into her hair, Deborah weaves a night of wonder.

Think like a queen. A queen is not afraid to fail. Failure is another stepping stone to greatness.
—OPRAH WINFREY, TALK SHOW HOST AND ACTRESS

You can't copy anybody and end up with anything. If you copy, it means you're working without any real feeling.
—BILLIE HOLIDAY, SINGER

Whether she's singing about watermelons or nightingales or dancing with her harp, she is mesmerizing, funny, and extremely talented. As *The Boston Globe* commented, "A night with Henson-Conant is some enchanted evening." Deborah sees this return to theater as an important turning point for her: "I'm doing something really different, which is actually crossing back to my roots in theater. I kept feeling like an impostor and telling myself that someday I would get back to writing musical theater, which was my first love—I wrote my first musical comedy when I was twelve—and I was completely unaware of the fact that I had already made that return. Everyone knew it but me. Even reviewers wrote that what I was doing on the concert stage was some form of music theater. I was the only one who couldn't see it. Then suddenly it hit me. I got into the theater, turned on the lights, and ahhhhhh, I was home."

Pam Moore, a partner in the international company Synectics, which does innovation consulting, took a series of intuitive U-turns in the course of her career path. She went to college to become a French teacher, noting that she grew up at a time when women had the choices of being a nurse, a teacher, or a secretary. In her sophomore year, she took a course called Voice and Articulation and, as a result, changed her major to speech pathology and received a fellowship for a master's degree. But during her clinical work, she realized that progress with clients was too slow and not interactive enough for her, so she left the program. She said it was hard to disappoint her family, but she trusted her intuition that she had to discover another route.

When you make a mistake, don't look back at it long. Take the reason of the thing into your mind, and then look forward. Mistakes are lessons of wisdom. The past cannot be changed. The future is yet in your power.
—MARY PICKFORD, ACTRESS

It takes courage to admit we're on the wrong train and risk disapproval or possibly looking foolish. For Pam, this ability to honor her truth was most wise. I can't tell you how many clients I've seen over the years who knew early on that they had chosen the wrong career but denied it.

Years later, with school loans and responsibilities, it is a much harder choice to undo. Like Joline, Pam's self-awareness that she was unhappy led her to a better match.

After leaving school, Pam taught dance at Arthur Murray and moved onto become a management trainee at Hilton Hotels for three years until she left in August 1972. Not knowing what was next, Pam answered a tiny ad in the paper one day that said, "Looking for creative people." The synchronicity of this story is remarkable—had Pam not opened the paper that one day in her search, her future could have been quite different. That ad was for Synectics, an innovation firm, where she was hired and now is an owner. After twenty-five years, Pam is an avid "Synector" and, like our other risk takers, is passionate about her work. Her face glows with joy as she says, "What inspires me is an incredibly profound belief that I'm not only creative but that I can help others discover their own creativity. We can all do it. The beauty is that we were all given the software. The problem is that over the years of needing to be right, we stopped using that muscle. Reawakening that potential still gives me goosebumps."

Fascination also affected the evolution of career guru Barbara Sher. Barbara invented a unique system of helping people make their wishes come true called "Success Teams." She lives by her words: "The good life is when you get up in the morning and can't wait to start all over again." Barbara radiates that kind of joy herself. Originally a counselor, she is particularly gifted in group dynamics, and it didn't take long before her career was booming.

Intrigued by people's stories, she proved to be a talented problem solver: "I wasn't interested in the medical model or disease of any kind. I just wanted to fix what was wrong so people could fly. I took one of these counseling groups and turned it into an early Success Team. It was by accident, but I saw what we could do when we helped each other achieve our personal goals and I watched people get well. And I was astonished. All we had to do was figure out what somebody wanted and then we'd all make sure they got it, whatever it was. We'd only work on people's feelings when they got anxious about going after their dreams. And I thought that's what this tool is for. You get untwisted so you can go do what you want. I wanted people who could write to write. I wanted people who could sing to sing. I wanted people to be happy and then move on."

Barbara then took her own advice. She was having so much fun with the accomplishments of her Success Teams that she created her own workshop and set off on her own. She made all of her friends come to her workshop, and they brought the media. After a year, she was discovered. She was written up in the *New York Times,* and five agents called to get her to write a book about her Success Teams, which became the bestselling *Wishcraft.*

Her Success Teams function like brainstorming-accountability-support groups. People come together regularly with the intent of meeting their own goals and promoting the goals of the other group members. They are powerful in the way that only groups can be. I first met Barbara back in the early 1980s, when my women's network group invited her to speak on Success Teams at our annual meeting. Barbara is a phenomenal speaker and facilitates a crowd like a pro. She exudes warmth and a passion for individual expression. As a participant, you not only have a great time but are inspired, entertained, and have your hope for humanity restored. As she is very much at peace with her own shortcomings, somehow she always makes you feel better about your own. For years I have recommended her books to clients, have been part of Success Teams myself, and was delighted that she wanted to do our interview.

Barbara is a petite powerhouse of a woman in her early sixties. She is cozy as an afghan yet adventurous and daring. She was just back from Turkey, having spent a month in a luxurious cave lined with Oriental rugs.

Books, not people, have been her mentors, and she has a special fondness for books by people who love mathematics and physics. Interested in everything, she experiences new places and ideas with wide-eyed wonder. Like me, she is a magazine addict and arrived with an armload of magazines on every possible topic. She loves writing and thinks words are "gorgeous." Her fascination with possibilities has transcended inferior teachers, unenlightened parents, unsupportive publishers, and monetary challenges. She is now internationally known. Her commitment to sharing what she knows and empowering others is a constant. Like Einstein, she discovered a formula that works, and she generously wants you to make use of it. Her new book, *It's Only Too Late If You Don't Start Now,* inspires people to embrace life after forty as a second chance. Barbara is living proof of the joy of fulfilling midlife dreams, since she published her first book at age forty-four.

Challenge: INTUITIVE MESSAGES

What messages are you receiving from your intuitive voice? Is your creative self inviting you to try new ventures? If so, which one(s)? Are you ready to follow your fascinations? If so, make a plan to take a positive risk. If you're holding back, what's stopping you—limited thinking, fear of disapproval, or moving outside of your secure comfort zone? What support do you need to take that positive risk and explore your intuitive leads?

Developing Staying Power

Shakti Gawain's blockbuster book *Creative Visualization* also began with Shakti's desire, like Barbara's, to share with others what she had learned from her explorations of human consciousness and personal growth. Her original vision was to write a very practical little booklet on visualization and market it to workshop participants and people on her mailing list. But the process didn't unfold easily, as Shakti says, "I sat down, all excited, and started to write enthusiastically. Then I hit a block—my inner critic. This inner critic said, 'Who do you think you are? What gives you the right to write a book telling people how to live their lives? Look at your life, it's not perfect.' My life was unfolding in quite an amazing way, but I didn't have a lot of material things. That critical voice stopped me. But I had sent out a little notice about this booklet to my mailing list of 200 people. I thought I would have it done soon, so I took orders and people sent in their $5. Well, I just started feeling guiltier and guiltier because all these people had sent in money and I was not producing this booklet. So eventually it was a combination of feeling obligated and my boyfriend saying, 'Hey, just do it' that got me to finish it. We printed it up, published it ourselves, and put it on consignment at some local metaphysical bookstores. When we came back, it was gone. It eventually became an underground hit."

Over the next several years, her book sold enough copies to get picked up by Bantam, and then she and her boyfriend started Whatever Publishing company. *Creative Visualization* has now sold over 2 million copies and has been translated into twenty-five languages. As Shakti says, "It's a total success story coming from me just following my impulse to want to share the things that were meaningful to me." By silencing that internal critic, Shakti wrote a life-changing book that started her on a career as a prolific author and workshop leader in the fields of intuition and personal growth. Her timing was impeccable—it put her on the forefront of the transpersonal movement. One could say her immediate success was "lucky." Yet they say that luck happens when preparation meets opportunity, and she had done her homework. Her readiness and the world's just clicked. I'm also struck by the power of her sense of responsibility to others. Shakti honored her commitment to her students and completed her book for their benefit.

Shakti's publishing company also published *The Shadow King: The Invisible Force That Holds Women Back,* a very important book for women written by psychologist Sidra Stone, Ph.D., which tells of her discovery of the presence of the Inner Patriarch in women. As Sidra says, "We carry within us an enemy we don't know about, who was passed down to us by our mothers." Sidra first became aware of this patriarchal voice when she noticed that the women in her workshop groups "lost themselves" when men showed up, even if they were in the midst of deep discussions and revelations. Using the Voice Dialogue technique that she and her husband Hal Stone created, Sidra began to talk to women's Inner Patriarchs and uncovered a whole world of devaluation of the feminine, all of which we carry within us.

The Inner Patriarch does not encourage women to take creative risks. Rather it torments us with limiting rules about our power, our relationships, and our sexuality and responsibility for the needs and wants of the men in our lives. Often, when we can't sustain the focus and discipline necessary to complete our creative projects, the Inner Patriarch inside of us is at work confusing us with "shoulds" and conflicting priorities. By uncovering this insidious voice inside of us, Sidra has identified a pathway to free our-

I want to do it because I want to do it. Women must try to do things as men have tried. When they fail, their failure must be but a challenge to others.
—AMELIA EARHART, AVIATRIX

selves from its tyranny. As Sidra says, "The negative impact of the Inner Patriarch is that he makes us children, acting like daughters to the men around us, and deprives us of real partnerships, and deprives men of real women."

Challenge: COMMUNICATING WITH YOUR INNER PATRIARCH

What did you learn from your mother and other women about limiting your self-expression? What are the primary messages that your internalized Inner Patriarch tells you about why you should defer to men? In what ways have you devalued the feminine in yourself and other women? How does your Inner Patriarch's voice hold you back from taking risks or following through on your creativity? Once you have uncovered the limitations on women preached by your inner patriarch, ask him or her to stand on the sidelines for a while so that you can experiment with your own power.

Often risk taking means doing what you think is right regardless of public opinion. Emmy-nominated actress and frequent star on on television shows, Christina Pickles, who played Drew Barrymore's mother in the recent hit film *The Wedding Singer,* graduated from the Royal Academy of Dramatic Art in England and came to America as a young actress. Christina is very much her own person and makes her own choices. For example, she decided to take an interesting role in *Nerds in Love IV,* even though as she says, "Some people would say, 'What a stupid thing to do.' I had a great time and it was a wonderful movie." She is very engaging on the screen and loves doing comedy. While Christina has a long list of credits, she is very up-front about how tough it is to make "a living wage" as an actress. Christina is also a very good acting teacher and enjoys it. As Christina tells her students, "The tragedy of being an actor in America is that you cannot survive on jobbing here or there. You have to have a series or you have to be a star. Monica Lewinsky has a much better chance of getting a series than any of you because we live in a culture of celebrity, not talent. There are thousands of men and women out there in the business who are not working." Inspired by newspapers and people's stories, Christina has also written and optioned several scripts, including a story from May Sarton. Yet, unlike many actors, Christina continues to work in her chosen field, and we will continue to see more of her since she is talented. One thing is clear: Christina is committed and won't give up.

Persistence is also an operating principle for Brenda Laurel, the vice president of design at Purple Moon, who started her career in speech and theater. In 1977, she added technology when she became a computer game designer. During the next twenty years, she developed expertise in technology research and design, and has now revolutionized entertainment software for girls. In 1992, with the support of Interval Research Corporation, Brenda spearheaded an exhaustive multimillion-dollar research project that studied the gender differences in play patterns and technology usage among children ages seven to twelve.

Four years later, Interval spun off a new company, Purple Moon, to develop and produce products they call "friendship adventures for girls," based on research Brenda guided. As she says, "Purple Moon's products capture what it means to be a girl today—deep friendships, a love of nature, the confidence to be yourself, and the courage to dream." Not surprising is the conclusion that success in these friendship adventure games is the development of relationships.

When I asked Brenda about the best career advice she ever got, she said, "It was to put my efforts where my mouth is. David Liddle of Interval encouraged me not to stand on the sidelines and make comments, but actually to try and do it. It's been harder than I thought and more rewarding than just about anything I could have imagined, too." Brenda's willingness to delve into the truth about gender differences in software entertainment has influenced a new generation of products that engage girls in both technology and personal development. As the mother of two daughters, Brenda knows the importance of this innovation. Since Purple

> The way I see it, if you want the rainbow, you gotta put up with the rain.
> —DOLLY PARTON, SINGER AND ACTRESS

Moon is a start-up company, there is always the risk of failure, but Brenda's creativity is sure to make this new product line succeed.

Heeding Your Heart

Janet Hagberg is a determined woman who keeps taking on bigger and more difficult risks. Attracted to "people on the fringe" who, she says, have been her best teachers, she volunteered at a prison several hours a month for fifteen years, including running a poetry group for women, and found she was especially attracted to women murderers. This led her on the path to healing domestic abuse. Janet says, "I learned a lot about survival and domestic violence at the prison. I don't think I would have been as drawn to this field, nor would I have learned about the silence surrounding abuse in my own family, if I hadn't bumped into women in prison who couldn't hide it. Most of us who were emotionally or physically battered are hiding it pretty well. But women in prison don't hide stuff. And if you go to prison, you find out what prison you're in."

Janet went on to become a spiritual director and wrote one of my favorite books on writing, *Wrestling with Your Angels: A Spiritual Journey to Great Writing*. She continues to write and to delve deeper into her truth, and says that her mission seems to be "to be vulnerable in print." She has pushed the edge of personal empowerment to societal empowerment. As cofounder of the Silent Witness National Initiative, based in Minneapolis, her program has three goals: the prevention of domestic violence, the safety of survivors, and the healing of perpetrators. On October 18, 1997, her organization marched 1,500 red wooden life-sized figures down the Mall in Washington, D.C., representing all of the women who were murdered during one year in the United States, victims of acts of domestic violence. Their goal is to heal domestic violence in this country and move to zero murders by the year 2010. In order to support this full-time volunteer commitment to social change, Janet gives two speeches a month on her book *Real Power* to pay her bills.

I mentioned to Janet that she just keeps outdoing herself, and she replied, "Can you put a scream into this story? I feel like if I'm obedient to what I feel called to do, I experience a deep level of peace inside of myself. So if you had asked me whether I would have chosen to be working on this national level in domestic violence, I would have said, 'Are you kidding me?' I want to read books, take walks, and watch college basketball. I don't want to do a national campaign because it's too hard. But here's where I am and I wouldn't choose to be anywhere else, because this is the obvious progression of my life journey. But I didn't sit down and set this goal."

Part of her process has been dealing with resistance, much of it from women. As Janet says, "Anytime you start looking at systems or moving up against them, you find out how powerful the shadow is in you and in the system too. There's a lot more shadow in me and out there than I thought, and that's been tough." Janet's spirituality guides her through these many challenges and supports her as she keeps moving to higher levels of trust and leadership.

Mystic Barrie Dolnick's creative path began while she was in advertising. As a midlevel account manager in a large Madison Avenue agency, she had the mindset that she was not "creative," despite the fact that she managed people, projects, and productions. "I let my job define me too much," remembers Barrie, "and let the outer world tell me when I was good or when I wasn't. To be a 'suit' in advertising, you have to be very creative, but I didn't realize or respect it at the time. After a few years, I started to hate my job, but as my salary climbed, I knew that it would be difficult to match my compensation in other fields."

Life intervened at the age of twenty-eight when Barrie's parents divorced, her serious relationship broke off, and she found herself working for a hostile boss. Barrie learned that this was what is called "Saturn return" in astrology, a time marked with challenges and hardship. While Barrie tried to switch careers at this point, she could not find anything to match her interests and, except for a fleeting attraction to the field of fund-raising for nonprofits, couldn't find a way out.

At this time a friend of Barrie's was taking a metaphysics class and encouraged her to attend. Barrie had to overcome some long-held resistance to give it a try: "When I was a really little girl, old women would come up to me and say that I had 'seeing eyes, ancient eyes,' but I hated that. I did have a lot of curiosity and I read books about past lives and other topics—but publicly I condemned it all as rubbish." Surrendering to her curiosity changed her life. Barrie learned about meditation, how to read tarot cards, and to do spells to conjure her true heart's desire.

"I was lucky. I asked for help and the universe sent me a friend. Out of the blue, this woman showed up to freelance at my agency. She became my mentor. She's an author in her own right and a copywriter. She told me to write a book but I didn't know what I could write about—or think that I'd have that much to say. I tried writing magazine articles, none of which were accepted. Then I met someone through my mother who had a contact at a big publishing company."

Using what Barrie calls her "passport"—reading tarot cards at business meetings—Barrie met with an editor, sold her first book idea, and then quit advertising. After a euphoric summer, the book deal fell through. "I started panicking. I think anybody who makes a great change in their life will reach the 'edge,' where you have no money, no faith, or no one will listen to you. In desperation, I thought, 'What can I do to get this book deal going again?' My mentor suggested that I get some press. So I used my advertising contacts and conjured up an idea. I called a former client of mine, one whose tarot cards I read with regularity, and asked if I could use her as a 'story,' since I had previously predicted the success of her new hotel with great accuracy. She came up with a better idea: offering my services as tarot reader and astrologer to the guests of her hotel. I became her press vehicle—the story ended up on the CBS network news, in *USA Today,* and in the *New York Times.* All of a sudden I had a television reel and a press kit, and I got another book deal in four seconds." Barrie has now published four books and founded her own business, Executive Mystic Services. Her traumatic Saturn return prompted her to release the wrong career and find her calling. Her background in advertising pays off to this day in that she knows how to market her ideas, and Barrie's books teach readers how to access their psychic power and hook up to the universe to manifest their own goals.

All of these women risked what was necessary to follow their fascinations. But, as they admit, stepping outside of the security of your comfort zone demands courage and the willingness to explore new possibilities. Calculated risks increase your chances for success because they are grounded in a plan. Yet, impulsive risks often tempt our creative whimsy and lead us onto a new playground. Just be sure to weigh the consequences before you surrender to your impulses. While learning to silence your doubts is an essential skill for a risk taker, life-threatening actions are not advised.

> A mistake is simply another way of doing things.
> —KATHERINE GRAHAM, PUBLISHER

All of the women in this book have stayed their course despite obstacles and failures. This perseverance breeds resilience, staying power that ultimately leads to success, unlike women who quit after one rejection or criticism.

To be a positive risk taker, you must practice, celebrate your victories, and grow from your mishaps. You must learn to become strong and trust yourself so you can persist in the wake of delays and detours. Fascinations have great power to keep us devoted and engaged. Follow your personal passions, take the necessary risks, and you will evolve.

Challenge: BOLSTERING YOUR STAYING POWER

How does limited thinking and/or the fear of being wrong or looking foolish short-circuit your creative goals? Noticing your beliefs about your creative ability will help you to stay afloat in the midst of a test of faith. What spiritual beliefs help or hinder you in taking chances, changing directions, trying something new and different, or charting your own course? Begin to collect examples of times when you have persevered and won. What skills or philosophy helped you to stay committed to your fascination despite obstacles? Identify and celebrate your strengths as a creative woman and a positive risk taker, and post them in your sanctuary.

SECRET 4

Surrendering to Creative Cycles

Experienced creative women know that their creativity moves in cycles of birth, death, and rebirth. Surrendering to the cycles instead of fighting with them is a skill of the creative warrior.

- Learning Patience
- Surviving the Void
- Navigating in the Darkness
- Watching for Clues
- Trusting in Creative Reemergence

There is this mysterious energy that
wants us to keep growing.

—MICHELLE CASSOU, ARTIST

Learning Patience

When I spoke with poet and writer Marilou Awiakta, she acknowledged being in a fallow season after devoting a decade to creating her book *Selu: Seeking the Corn Mother's Wisdom.* As she says, "After writing *Selu,* I gave another five years to traveling and planting seed-thoughts: telling people the traditional Cherokee story of Selu, exchanging ideas about how to apply her teachings to contemporary issues, and asking people to connect the Corn-Mother's wisdom to kindred teachings in their own heritage. I listen a lot, and this communal season is very important in my creative cycle. Now I'm lying fallow—resting, reassessing, and waiting for my new work to take root." I asked her if she was confident that the next idea would show up when the time was right and she agreed, "Yes, it always does. I just stay in a state of readiness and listening. I know if I push, if I should get a frantic feeling, it will make the idea slower in coming."

There is an old Viking divination system called the runes. When troubled with a question, for guidance you can draw one of twenty-five stones, each inscribed with a symbol. Awiakta's statement reminds me of the Harvest rune, which is subtitled, "Fertile Season, One Year." Ralph Blum, author of *The Book of Runes,* describes the Harvest stone in this way: "Remember the farmer who was so eager to assist his crops that he went out at night and tugged on the new shoots. There is no way to push the river; equally you cannot hasten the harvest. Be mindful that patience is essential for the recognition of your own process which, in its season, leads to the harvest of the self." Many times when I am lusting for results or assured, speedy outcomes, this rune sobers up my impatience. Awiakta's use of the word *fallow* for the void reminds us that farmland was allowed to rest between crops when we lived in an agrarian culture. Nature always reminds us of the natural order of both dormancy and blossoming.

In her writings and teachings, Awiakta uniquely fuses three heritages: Cherokee, Appalachian, and the scientific high-tech world. "This fusion comes naturally to me because I grew up on a reservation for atoms, not Indians, in Oak Ridge, Tennessee. During the 1940s and '50s, the city was a secret nuclear research center. From childhood, science was part of my everyday life. My fusion of science with the Cherokee traditional story of Selu is of ancient origin. Like other indigenous peoples, the Cherokee based their sacred stories on centuries of experience with nature's laws. Selu teaches the Law of Respect, the law that helps people live in balance and harmony with nature and with each other—when you take, you have to give back."

Surviving the Void

In the creative cycles of birth and death and rebirth, there are times when we are empty of ideas, adrift in a sea of ambiguity and nothingness. These times can be labeled the neutral zone, the void, a vacuum. No matter what they are called, they are part of the creative cycle, and wise women accept them and trust that when it's time, their inspirations will percolate again. This void beckons like a doorway to transformation and new beginnings. Yet fear can be a fellow traveler on this path to who knows where. Surviving in the void demands a range of skills: being willing to let go, staying in the dark long enough, nurturing your visions and dreams, following the clues as they present themselves, remaining true to yourself, and having the belief that something will appear. The void often feels like a test. It may be escorted in by job loss, illness, death, betrayal, burnout, disillusionment, or other life crises we didn't sign up for. While we long to restore the old, its time has passed, even if we wish otherwise. Such passages force us to redesign our internal selves and often produce surprising results. But they also involve loss, grief, and despair, as well as communion with our darker side. Change thrusts us into chaos, and it takes time to reorder things and find a new route. Courage is mandatory.

I fear the venture into the unknown. But that is part of the act of creating and the art of performing.
—Martha Graham,
DANCER

I've encountered the void numerous times in the course of my life. But my chronic fatigue syndrome pulled me down into the void like nothing else. I kept trying to move on, but my body pulled me back. During the height of my illness, without fail, I kept drawing the runes Disruption, Standstill, and Constraint. All my plans were disrupted, my life was frozen at a standstill, and everywhere around me I felt limitations and a sense of being held back. Every time I tried to force myself forward, I was hurled back to bed.

I had to release my old life and my outgrown self. I could no longer take care of everyone else; my energy was being pulled inward to delineate my own needs on all levels. My life had to be rebalanced and more sharply focused on what I truly wanted to do and be. You can't hide from the void—it envelops you and keeps pulling you under like a relentless octopus. When you have discovered your truth, though, the creature lets go.

In this vacuum of the neutral zone, we can be lost for long stretches until we connect with what truly excites us. Art therapist and author Lucia Capacchione says, "When I got sick in 1973, my whole life turned around and gave me the career I have now. That's when I started keeping my journal. My body said, 'Hey if you're going to stay out there as an extrovert, that's fine, but we're going to make it impossible. We body parts are going to break down. You've got to sit in bed and be quiet now.' These were the kind of dialogues I had with my body. It was inevitable that if I was going to be healthy I had to balance out." For Lucia, this battle with her health led to writing her first series of books and training as an art therapist. The void pushed her into a personal healing journey and the development of books and workshops that now heal others.

Life intervened also for Sarah Ban Breathnach. For so many of us, "time out" from our busy chaotic lives allows for the alignment necessary to tap into our dormant creativity. It's the inner centering that pollinates the new. For Sarah, it was a sudden accident: "My daughter and I were in a fast food restaurant and we were just biting into our hamburgers, and a large ceiling panel fell and hit me on the head and knocked me onto the table. If it had hit Katie, it would have killed her. Thank God, it just grazed her eye. But I suffered a head injury and I was partially disabled for

> Life shrinks or expands in proportion to one's courage.
> —ANÄIS NIN,
> WRITER

seventeen months. For the first three months I was confined to bed as I lost the use of my senses. I really thought my writing career was over, because I couldn't even read—I taught myself to read again with Katie's books.

"Because I was a journalist and radio broadcaster, we had to keep this quiet. But it was that seventeen months of recovery that enabled me to think about how much I really loved the Victorian era. When I was getting better, I decided to start doing workshops on Victorian traditions. I called them 'Mrs. Sharp's Traditions' and I began writing again. But during that time of head injury, there were very, very dark days and I wondered what I was going to do with the rest of my life."

The tragedy led Sarah to reconnect with the actress in her as a workshop leader, and to the publication of her first two books on the Victorian era, essential steps on the path to writing *Simple Abundance*. Her third book was meant to be on Victorian decorative details, but her creative flow stopped. Sarah had no energy to write it, so she let it go. Letting go and seeing what we're really drawn to fertilizes the creative process, and finally the next step appears. Sarah still had not claimed her authentic voice and was writing from the mindset of the 125-year-old character of Mrs. Sharp. When she hit the void again, an astounding personal transformation unfolded for Sarah, culminating in her strong spiritual voice in the bestseller *Simple Abundance* and her new book *Something More*.

In our linear culture, these episodes of disruption, time out, feeling lost, or time off are viewed suspiciously. Yet life is a series of cycles and was never meant to roll out on a straight line. For many years academia and enlightened organizations have encouraged people to take sabbaticals to explore new interests, complete a project, or recharge their batteries. Entrepreneur Joline Godfrey and her former business partner had a corporate policy of taking at least one week's vacation each quarter. Joline's policy confirms what I strongly believe, which is that ideas are often born when we have time off and peace of mind. Corporate America could benefit from this insight, especially in the midst of the current workaholic madness.

> When you get into a tight place and everything goes against you until it seems that you cannot hold on for a minute longer, never give up then, for that is just the place and time when the tide will turn.
>
> —HARRIET BEECHER STOWE, WRITER

The full life is filled with vulnerability, not defense.... You face whatever feeling there is.

—VIRGINIA SATIR,
FAMILY THERAPIST

Burnout is a key enemy of innovation. Leisure time and the inspiration of a new location helped Joline to recreate herself after the sale of her first business. "When I moved from Boston to California, I moved here cold," she said. "I didn't know a single person. I just knew that I needed new perspective. I hadn't a clue what I was going to do next. And yet I understood that the only way I could really find my direction was to put myself in a situation where something else could appear on the horizon. A friend of mine described it as falling out of an airplane without a parachute, and that really is what it has been like at many points in my life. But I'm old enough and experienced enough to see that if you just trust the universe—and that's so trite and New Age sounding—things have a way of working out in a better way. I'm probably happier and healthier more often than a lot of my friends who don't live their lives that way."

As much as she loves her work, Pam Moore still responds to her inner cycles. Last year, she gave herself a yearlong sabbatical from her beloved Synectics and cooked, gardened, and was a "wife to my husband." In addition, she has repositioned herself at Synectics so that she can focus on her fascination with product naming and cultivate many of the ideas on creativity that have been beckoning her for years. Like Pam, responding to our needs for rest and new experiences reigns as a key requisite in fueling our creative cycle.

Illness and accidents can precipitate these passages, but letting go of an unsatisfactory life circumstance is also a major doorway. As a career coach, people often ask me if it's wise to leave a job or a business they despise before they have another job or business plan developed. Ideally, going from one sure thing to the next can be a financially sound principle. Yet for people who are burned out, who are doing work that's harmful to their well-being or being victimized by a crazy manager, staying in that situation compromises not only their self-worth but also their ability to create a new vision for a positive future.

For many people, releasing themselves from a pathological bondage and investing time in their development pays off profoundly. Taking the opportunity to get clear on a new direction can save you a lot of backtracking or heartache later. Often transfor-

The fullness of life is in the hazards of life.

—EDITH HAMILTON,
WRITER

mation cannot begin without this willingness to liberate ourselves from what's impeding our growth and happiness.

Creativity consultant C. Diane Ealy claims that trusting her own truth helps her to minimize fear and keep moving. She also says, "The realization I had a few years ago is that when I am feeling fearful about something in terms of my own personal growth, then I know I'm on the right track." This fits with Diane's "Ealy's Roller Coaster Theory," which says, "Fear and excitement are the same emotion; they are just experienced from a different perspective. With a roller coaster, anybody in their right mind starts out fearful. But after the roller coaster takes you to the top of that first hill, it shifts that fear into excitement. If it didn't do that, nobody would get back on." Understanding this dynamic helps Diane to focus on her enthusiasm about a challenge.

Many spiritual teachings like *A Course in Miracles* contend that there are only two emotions—love and fear. You can't experience both at once. This is where the catalyst of passion, a form of love, makes the difference. When we are passionate about something like a dance or a song or a client, then we choose to transcend the fear. The excitement of the goal overrules our self-doubt and terror. Harnessing that power is key to moving up to the summit of creativity.

Challenge: DEALING WITH THE VOID

Have you ever felt stuck and lost? How did you handle it? What has been your life pattern of creative cycles? What helps you to manage the void? What have been the important catalysts that moved you into the next cycle?

Navigating in the Darkness

Whenever and however we arrive at the void, the experience promises to give us a close encounter with fear and insecurity. As we release an old identity and move into a sense of being lost, purposeless, undefined, or confused, we must encounter the darkness in ourselves. Marilyn Veltrop tells of such a time. Many years ago in Peru, she impulsively raised her hand to volunteer as a guide.

This experience changed her life forever. "I was on this shaman's journey, and there was a middle of the night ceremony involving a Cave of the Dark and a Cave of the Light. Our leader asked for volunteers to serves as guides into the Caves. I found myself, without thinking at all, immediately raising my hand to guide people into the Cave of the Dark. Somehow I knew I had to do it. It was really important to me. So first of all, I went in and stood near the opening of the cave by myself. And there were all of these grotesque images that I was experiencing in the upper part of the cave. Initially, it was a scary process where I wondered what I had gotten myself into. And then I looked over at the far end of the cave and there was a translucent blue eagle, just sitting there very calmly. I immediately felt at peace and strengthened. The eagle showed up for me as a power animal in Peru. Following that, each person in my group was led to the entrance of the Cave; then I would guide them into the interior, leave them to have their own experience for a while, and go get them to bring them back. People went through some pretty heavy-duty stuff while they were in there. I stood on guard for them.

"It wasn't until sometime later, when I was reading about Persephone's becoming Queen of the Underworld and guiding others into the underworld and back, that I realized what that experience was about for me in Peru." Marilyn now believes that she was called to California by Persephone to study at the Institute of Transpersonal Psychology and become a transformational coach and guide to others.

In her painting workshops, Michelle Cassou encourages you to move into the unknown. As she says, "To be creative means becoming more familiar with being a little lost. If we are always full of what we want to do, there is no room for the new." She reminds us that it is the process that counts, not the painting. Michelle is also a great believer in cycles and explains, "Creation comes from cycles—sometimes small waves and sometimes big waves. And as the waves end, they want to rest—they have given all they could and need to replenish before moving again. The waves need time to build up again. I find that in painting, writing, in everything creative, that we move in cycles. We never go to a

When you come to the edge of all the light you know, and are about to step off into the darkness of the unknown, faith is knowing one of two things will happen: There will be something solid to stand on, or you will be taught how to fly.

—BARBARA WINTER,
WRITER

space that's just the same. The way to grow is to keep creating and letting go of what we hold onto and moving more into the spontaneous and the intuitive realm."

Being willing to be in the unknown helped Carol Frenier create her book *Business and the Feminine Principle* in fall 1994. But she had no idea that she was birthing a book. She only had a sense that she wanted to write some essays derived from her journals. As she says, "I needed to tinker with my material. It was a wonderful process. I would get lost. All time would stop. I wouldn't think about anything else going on in my life. I would just really be in it, and I discovered that for me that was an exquisite place to be. So I went back through all of my writings and I ended up with a bunch of files with loose headings. I had this cluster of paragraphs, none of which had any relation to each other. When I saw a connection, I would stop my sorting process and just play with it. After eight months of doing this, I came across an old journal entry that blew me away. I had made a notation that I wanted to write a book called *Seeds of Thought*. And here I was five years later, actually doing it." While the title of her book ultimately changed, playing in her maze of seemingly unrelated ideas led Carol to fashion a completely new entity. Her passion for the ideas outweighed the fear she felt about not knowing what she was doing.

Challenge: PASSION AS AN ANTIDOTE TO FEAR

1. Think of a time when you wanted something so much that you were willing to do anything to get it. What was the outcome?

2. Do you feel exhilarated by your creative work right now? What ignites you the most about it? If you're not psyched about your current work, what would you rather be doing?

3. What discomfort are you willing to endure to promote and experience your passion?

4. What are your specific fears about yourself and your work?

Visualize a seesaw with your work as the fulcrum of the board. Label one side of the seesaw "fear" and label the other side "excitement," and notice how balanced or imbalanced the board is. Now go to the fear seat, raise yourself up high, and imagine sending all of your fears of rejection and criticism down to the excitement side. Let them just slide down the board and stay there. Then go to the excitement seat and enjoy its energy and potency. Imagine being able to live in that place of excitement with fear at bay. Notice any creative insights that occur to you while you are in that excitement seat. This exercise can be very helpful for decision making, as sometimes the fear seat warns us against a justified hazard that we would be wise to avoid. Play with this seesaw image and allow yourself to be more in control of your choices.

Watching for Clues

Transformational guide Marilyn Veltrop's experience in the year before she left Boston illustrates the power of readiness. Everything Marilyn tried to initiate that year, whether new relationships, a meaningful graduate program, or work projects, failed. She kept saying that she wanted to be out in nature and be "hugged by trees." So, she sold her beloved condo because she knew it was time and rented a house in the woods that had been on the market for a long while—but the house sold shortly after she unpacked. As Marilyn remembers, "I just felt this huge sense of betrayal. I was depressed, disillusioned, and really confused. I didn't know where I was headed. It was like everything was falling apart. I was hitting deadends all over the place."

Marilyn sought guidance for herself from Ashtiana, a psychic in New York whom Marilyn had consulted before, and told her that nothing was working. Ashtiana looked her in the eye and said, "You don't get it yet, do you? You don't belong here anymore." In that moment Marilyn says, "Those words resonated through my whole body and spoke the truth that I had not yet been able to see. Suddenly, the failures and the endings of the previous year made sense—they were clearing space for a major move." Less than six months later, Marilyn relocated to California and began her graduate study. Marilyn's journey has been a formidable element in helping me to understand that when things aren't working, we need to pay attention to the underlying message we may be missing.

The universe affirmed Marilyn's decision to move cross-country and supported her in making a smooth transition. In fact, within two years, she had manifested most of her vision from her Boston days, including a life/work partner who is now her husband, and a home in a beautiful natural setting overlooking Monterey Bay.

But the descents continued, and went deeper and deeper: "Once I came out here, my journey took me through several more intensive descents, which involved going into the void over and over again. Given that an important part of my work is to serve as a guide to others into the Underworld and back, it just demanded that I go through descents repeatedly myself as part of my preparation." Her dissertation, which will one day be a book, shifted from being a project about leadership to being a project about the transformational journeys of business leaders. In working with her own intuitive cues, Marilyn was able to find her real purpose.

Dancer Leslie Neal believes strongly in surrendering to the void. She often has no real idea where she's going to end up when she begins choreographing, but watches for the signals as the movements unfold. She appreciates the freedom to do her art, which is dance, without the need for her creative work to provide her sole means of financial security, which comes from her professorship. As the leader of a dance theater company, Leslie can freely step into the unknown and create: "I've been fortunate to work with a group of dancers who are willing to explore. My process is to take risks and have faith. I search out themes from the chaos, even if I'm not sure where I'm going. So it's always been a process of discovery. In many ways, the work makes itself. It emerges from deep within the subconscious, and begins to reveal itself. Sometimes it's a painful and emotional journey, but it's always transformative. I tend to work best with women, and we bring ourselves and our

> Diamonds are only chunks of coal that stuck to their jobs, you see.
> —MINNIE RICHARD SMITH, POET

67

lives fully into the studio. Our work is shaped from our collective experience and in that way, it's very collaborative and healing."

Sometimes, the signs of new beginnings appear, but we have to get rid of the interference that is standing in the way of our recognizing them. Carmella Yager, a talented painter and teacher, longs for a grant that will allow her to do a series of paintings on bottles, bodies, and embodiment. Yet as a committed and conscientious teacher who gives her students permission to find their inner light, Carmella has a dilemma about how to make room for this new growth. Recently, while painting in Spain, Carmella noticed her freedom from the voices of her students and friends. When she returned she detected the difference: "I didn't even think about it until I got back and I tried to paint here. And it's like, who's in my head? They weren't here in Spain—they were gone. Now they're all back. A lot of them are students and dear friends, but it's not time for them to be here. Before it was the critic in my head but now it's people that I love. But I need space in my head. I'm ready now to just burrow down for a year, not go anywhere and not see anyone."

Sometimes signs beckon from our dreams. Designer Diane Ericson thrives on pushing the creative edge and carrying others with her to their own ledge of discovery. In the depths of one of her void cycles, after her husband left, Diane had a life-changing dream about letting go: "I was standing in front of a big Coliseum-shaped building that was curving away from me and it had hundreds of doors all the way around the bottom. All the doors were totally open, but I couldn't get through them because I had two huge bags in my hands. With my hands tightly holding onto those bags, I was running from door to door trying to contort my body and pull or push the bags through at different angles. Then I heard a little voice say, 'Drop the bags, drop the bags.' And I let go. I could feel my arms release. Not only could I walk through any of the doors, but the entire wall melted, just like a Dali painting. In front of me was this huge open field that was just oozing with everything that was rich and abundant. This dream reminded me that everything I needed was always there." As with Diane, surrendering to our challenges instead of denying them or struggling with them spells victory for our creative transforming self. Change is like a river that flows through each of our lives, and we need to learn to navigate its nuances. Diane now sees life's twists and turns as redesign opportunities, and that is what she teaches her students. Fighting against the cycles is fruitless; leveraging the clues in each cycle propels us forward.

Trusting in Creative Reemergence

In one of my bookstore meanderings, I discovered Lesley Shore's first book *Healing the Feminine: Reclaiming Woman's Voice*. I loved this book, and I found out that she lives on Harmony Farm about twenty miles from me. I called her, and she agreed to meet with me. Harmony Farm is a charming haven with wildflowers and rare medicinal herbs, woods, and tranquility. It reminded me of my beloved childhood forest. Lesley is a clinical psychologist as well as a writer and has a long history of activism on women's issues. In fact, she was one of the founders of an organization in Boston called Women's Lodge, where I had attended a few meetings, so our paths had unknowingly crossed before. Lesley grew up in England with parents who liked art. Her mother was a potter, her maternal grandmother was a pianist, and she has an art therapist cousin in England who knows the ways of the mushroom. Each of these women inspired her.

Lesley's first book grew out of a vacuum, but it was sparked by the impetus from two other women. Lesley had a friend in Michigan who was beginning a novel, and her friend's intention planted seed number one. This was followed by a comment from a colleague who reminded Lesley that she had always planned to write a book.

Lesley began by freeing up several mornings. As she says, "I cleared out some space, shifted some clients, and made the time even though I really didn't know if I was going to do anything." I asked her if it was hard to keep her commitment and she said "No." She had long been involved in women's issues and was guided to write what she knew, so her books emerged. Her second book, called *Tending Inner Gardens: The Healing Art of Feminist Psychotherapy*, uses her love of plants as a dominant metaphor.

At the time I met with Lesley, she had spent the previous year researching her family's Holocaust story but had decided that she

> I wanted to be scared again.... I wanted to feel unsure again. That's the only way I learn, the only way I feel challenged.
> —CONNIE CHUNG, BROADCASTER

wouldn't publish it until the people involved were gone. She felt like she just needed to garden and to learn about the medicinal herbs that were currently being overharvested, and which she passionately wanted to protect. I asked her if she thought she'd write about these herbs, and her response reflects her state of total openness: "I don't know. I'm not deciding where I'm going. To be perfectly honest, I'm in transition and I'm allowing the transition to be a transition. After my two books, I got involved in several women's and editing projects. And now I've resigned from everything. So whether what's next is in the books or the gardens, I don't know. I think something else will be happening on the other side of this transition, but I'm not quite sure what. I think it'll somehow happen at Harmony Farm."

When I checked with Lesley more than a year later, she told me she had been studying herbs, making herb gardens, renovating a pond, and considered herself "Earth steward" of Harmony Farm. As Lesley exemplifies, women who have been intimate with the creative process and created pots or books or prints or whatever, have a confidence in the cycles and the inevitability of the emergence of the new. Creative passions have come and gone, and therefore there is faith that inspirations will once again emerge.

There is another cycle women have to consider when tapping into their creativity, and that is matching up their creative work cycles with the stages of their children's lives. The cycles of parenting or other caretaking may either fuel or interrupt the flow. Many women have said to me that they could never have reached the creative heights they have when their children were young. Still others say that having children actually sparked new creative cycles for them. No one can say what's true for you—we are all individuals with our own unique reactions to life events.

However it is ushered in, change has an impact on us as a creative vessel. Aligning ourselves with what life bestows upon us, accepting the inevitability of endings and emptiness, and envisioning new heights of growth and achievement honors the cycles of death and rebirth. We all need time between cycles to rest and fill ourselves up again with fresh dreams and energy.

All that is necessary to break the spell of inertia and frustration is this: Act as if it were impossible to fail.
—DORTHEA BRANDE, WRITER

Challenge: FUELING YOUR CYCLES

What stimulates your creativity into its highs and lows? Keep an ongoing excitement list and watch how it changes. Write down anything that attracts you to it and why, and notice the shifts over time. On a regular basis, try new things and see what comes up for you. Change your routes, your rooms, your restaurants, your rituals, and see what unique connections emerge. Fortify your ability to handle change.

Congratulations. You have now completed your work in the First Gateway.

Second Gateway

Mastering Your Challenges as a Creative Woman

*"How does one become a butterfly?" she asked pensively.
"You must want to fly so much that you are willing
to give up being a caterpillar."*

—TRINA PAULUS, WRITER

Committing to Self-Focus

Self-focus is a critical skill for women who want to create. Without it, you cannot indulge in your inspirations and devote the time necessary for innovation.

 Keys:

- Confronting Fears of Selfishness
- Putting Yourself on Top of the Priority List
- Honoring Your Holistic Style
- Setting Boundaries
- Creating Solitude
- Supporting Self-focus in Other Women

A woman must find her own voice.

MAUREEN MURDOCK, *THE HEROINE'S JOURNEY*

*N*umerous people have challenged me about why I am writing a book focused only on creative women. I've heard barbs like, "Aren't men creative too?" Of course they are. Men like Elton John, Steven Spielberg, Bill Gates, and Louis Rukeyser are among the millions of exceptionally creative men in our midst. Like women, many men abandon their creative passions as well. Between feeling the shackles of their social conditioning to be the primary breadwinners in their families and the pressure to choose macho careers, men may also fear choosing the creative path. But that's another book. While men have their own demons to overcome, women must tackle centuries of societal conditioning and psychological conflicts in order to give high priority to their creative work.

Not all women agree. A famous novelist, when invited to participate in this book, disagreed with my premise to interview just women. In a lovely letter, she declined to participate and wrote, "My resistance has to do with the fact that, for the last several years, I've consistently declined to be included in any project that's gender-segregated. It's been my experience that women are hindered and misled by such distinctions. I've maintained for years that writing has nothing to do with gender and that also applies to the notion of creativity in its broader sense. The work is the work and it has nothing to do with the artist's being male or female. Addressing such questions as if there were a difference between the sexes does women a disservice and it's something I can't bring myself to support."

I must disagree. My inner knowing and witness to the struggles of my women friends and clients supports a totally different reality. If you review the life stories of famous creative men throughout history, most have been blessed with wives and helpers to handle the details of their lives so that they could work undisturbed and easily maintain their connection with the creative process. Women and children tiptoed around these men, left meals outside their doors, critiqued, edited, and managed their business needs. These men's careers flourished with all that support. In addition, society generally didn't judge them for abdicating their "true responsibility" of caring for others.

Self-focus presents many challenges unique to women. As we have seen in the previous four chapters, the *self* is the conduit of creative energy. Thus, in order to birth creative awareness, self-focus is an essential state of mind. The creative process is a dance between the self and a medium; therefore, the self must be free for immersion in the sensations and the steps.

In her essay "On the Creative Necessity of Sacrifice" in *Women, Creativity, and the Arts,* Diane Apostolos-Cappadona speaks to this dilemma: "The problem is the simple reality that the act of writing a poem or a novel, of painting a picture, of sculpting a form, of choreographing a dance, of composing an étude is not a simple or time-bounded activity. Rather, it requires a total commitment of energies and attention, and an ability to suspend time and space—eureka, the heart of the problem for creative women, whose total attention would be shifted away from their home and children to their art!" Because of our societal script to care for others, this decision to engross ourselves totally in our creative work, even in time-limited segments, generates more conflicts for most women than it does for men.

> Eternally, woman spills herself away in driblets to the thirsty, seldom being allowed the time, the quiet, the peace, to let the pitcher fill up to the brim.
>
> —ANNE MORROW LINDBERGH, WRITER

Confronting Fears of Selfishness

Many women fear appearing or actually being selfish if they commit to their creative work. They say things like, "People will feel like I'm a bad mother if I get too serious about my work," "When I work intensely, I neglect my house and my husband," "It's not a woman's role to be so work-focused and self-indulgent," and "I'll never attract a lover if I achieve too much with my art." This dread of being accused of selfishness continues to keep us in our place. As psychologist Lesley Shore says in *Healing the Feminine: Reclaiming Woman's Voice,* "A 'feminine' woman is supposed to be self-denying and self-sacrificing. While we have supposedly graduated from being servants, we are still expected to serve others, to minister to their needs." Lesley herself said that she couldn't have written her two books with children living at home; writing had to wait until they were grown.

Some of the women profiled in this book have even avoided intimate partnerships, especially with men, as they didn't trust that their creative expression could flourish in that traditional feminine role.

There is a myth that says that really creative women are impossible and difficult people. For so many women of previous generations, especially artists, devotion to their work meant madness and/or isolation. Women today are seeking to merge passionate work with love relationships and often children, too. So today's creative woman is careful about her choice of partner. As artist and writer Lucia Capacchione says, "One of the things I have found draining over the years has been relationships with men who were in any way threatened by my creative process. I find I cannot tolerate that dynamic. The problem with my last two relationships was that when the chips were down, they couldn't handle my creativity and so I exited." In order to activate your creativity, your creative expression must be given priority status—most important, by you. You must be a warrior with those around you to insist that they support you.

As girls, too many of us learned that "being selfish" was a sin. If we didn't want to share our doll or our treehouse with someone else, we were surely a wicked little girl. Barbara Waugh, worldwide personnel manager for Hewlett-Packard Labs, longtime activist for human rights, and a woman who has dedicated her life to serving others, recalls her fear of being labeled selfish: "I was the oldest of four children with a dad who was a pilot and never home. When I would sit and read or disappear, then my mom didn't have anybody to help her. I learned that focusing on myself was not the right choice. I think the other thing that kicks in is that you get lots of rewards for taking care of everybody else."

The truth is that selfishness has had a bad rap. In her book *The Virtue of Selfishness,* Ayn Rand writes, "In popular usage, the word 'selfishness' is a synonym of evil; the image it conjures up is

> It is easier to live through someone else than to become complete yourself.
>
> —BETTY FRIEDAN, WOMEN'S ADVOCATE

of a murderous brute who tramples over piles of corpses to achieve his own ends, who cares for no living being and pursues nothing but the gratification of the mindless whims of any immediate moment. Yet the exact meaning and dictionary definition of the word 'selfishness' is: *concern with one's own interests*. This concept does not include a moral evaluation."

It is appropriate for all of us, men and women, to be concerned with our own interests. The seeds of child abuse are often sown in parents who deny their own needs. Women who sacrifice their own fulfillment for their children are often angry and depressed, and may take these seething emotions out on their offspring. Also, modeling martyrdom does not teach our daughters how to be happy, authentic women. A healthy family is a mutual collaboration with a commitment to the well-being of each individual, including all the women. For many women, a creative outlet while raising children protects her and her children from great unhappiness and stress. Self-fulfilled people have more positive energy available for the challenges of parenting. This continues to be a particular problem for women. Are creative men condemned to the label of selfishness as often as women are? Rarely. If a child is having problems, for example, very few people would advise the father to quit his job, whereas a woman would be held accountable for pursuing her own interests, and possibly neglecting her child.

The truth is that *some creative men and women are irresponsible and neglectful of friends and family, and some aren't.* "Narcissistic" is really a better word to use than "selfish." Narcissism means "self-love; excessive interest in one's own appearance, comfort, importance, abilities." The key word here is *excessive.*

Narcissistic people often don't take care of others to whom they are responsible. In the case of parenting, ignoring a screaming baby or not supervising a wandering toddler is certainly reckless behavior for any parent. Not being willing to listen to and comfort a friend undermines the integrity of that relationship. But how many men are tortured by the terror that they will be judged as selfish if they decide to become an accomplished composer, start a bakery, or cultivate the perfect lawn?

Self-reliance is the only road to true freedom, and being one's own person is its ultimate reward.
—PATRICIA SAMPSON, WRITER

As far as I can see from here almost everyone I know is trying to do the impossible every day. All mothers, all writers, all artists of every kind, every human being who has work to do and still wants to stay human and to be responsive to another human being's needs, joys, and sorrows. There is never enough time and that's the rub. In my case every choice I make means depriving someone.
—MAY SARTON, WRITER

As individual women, we must devise a plan that balances our creative urges with our responsibilities to others. For example, a friend of mine hires a baby-sitter two days a week so she can work on a new software design. That way she doesn't have to postpone her creative genius *and* her children are well cared for. On Saturdays, her husband takes the kids on errand "adventures" all day.

Enlightened couples these days are seeking to design lives based on equality, where each partner has more license to express his or her creativity, and parenting/caretaking is handled more as a joint effort rather than the total domain of the woman. It is heartening to note the number of men who are now resisting the workaholic norm or changing careers to spend more time with their families. This is an extraordinary revolution for both men and women and their children. But these are still experimental relationships haunted by the ghosts of the past. For women in loving lesbian relationships, shared empowerment is usually a founding principle of the relationship, so there are usually fewer issues about equality to wrestle through.

As women, we all grew up in a patriarchal culture whose toxic threads still permeate our conscious and unconscious actions. I have always been fascinated by the power of context. In fact, in my early twenties, when I was deciding whether to become a psychologist or a clinical social worker, I chose the social work route because of its emphasis on helping people *within the context of their lives and their culture.* While we women are a diverse group collectively, we grew up in a patriarchal culture riddled with the learnings from our mothers and female role models. Many of us learned as young girls to let the boys win and to play a seductive second. That's a powerful axiom to shatter. Even though the outside world has changed and women are freer to make their own choices, for many of us, those messages about our role in society and the devaluation of women still haunt us.

As Sidra Stone says in *The Shadow King: The Invisible Force That Holds Women Back,* "As I came to know my own Inner Patriarch and those of other women, a clear pattern emerged. I could see how our Patriarchs keep us in an inferior position—if not

in our work, then in our relationships. They make us distrust ourselves. Even more important was the discovery that they make us
distrust other women as well.... I saw again and again how the
Inner Patriarch devalued us and what we did just because we were
women." If we disbelieve our own intuition and inspirations, then
avoiding creative challenges becomes a safer route than risking to
venture into the imaginative land of surprises, rerouting, and, yes,
dead ends and rejections. But when we deny our creative urges for
fear of being selfish, we risk living our whole lives without ever
cultivating and offering the gifts that are ours alone to give to the
world.

Challenge: YOUR SELFISHNESS ISSUES

What did you learn about being "selfish" as a child? What did
your mother teach you about your role(s) as a woman?
Do you have any unfinished business with your mother about
either not being taken care of or being smothered? How do you
distinguish a self-focused woman from a narcissistic woman?

Putting Yourself on Top of the Priority List

With our multiple roles and responsibilities as caretakers of relationships, too many women have learned to become a "type E"
woman—as in everything for everyone else first. The type E
woman rarely gets out of the creative starting gate because there is
always something else to do for someone else at every moment.
Being overly involved in the lives of others can actually be an escape
from testing out our own creative power. Too many talented women
have stayed hidden at home, too scared to gamble on themselves. As
Sidra and I discussed extensively, women have learned that our
needs are secondary and that our creative efforts are frivolous simply because we are women. Most men are not burdened with these
same handcuffs from the culture. As Sidra says, "In fulfilling this
role of caregiver and the protector of relationship and family,
women have learned to move beyond their own needs to meet the
needs of others. This has been creative and quite wonderful in many

I have no regrets.
I wouldn't have lived
my life the way I did
if I was going to
worry about what
other people were
going to say.
—INGRID BERGMAN,
ACTRESS

ways, but women have paid a high price. We have lost our ability to make choices, to know what it is that we want, and to think for ourselves. It feels as though in the realm of the Shadow King, there is a law that says 'Others come first.' Women can only do as they wish after everyone else has been cared for."

To achieve creatively, we must shift our *other* orientation into communication with *self*. One way to do this is to put yourself on the list of people you are committed to support. You are probably great at nurturing others—don't you deserve the same quality care from yourself? Your creativity has to be a priority for you before anyone else will take you seriously.

Activist Barbara Waugh recently went to Hawaii where a friend strongly urged her to meet with the Hawaiian elder Auntie Abby: "My friend dropped me off in the park with Auntie Abby, and Auntie Abby reached over and took my hand in kind of a death grip. She looked me in the eye and said, 'You are lost. You don't know who you are or what you want. You run around taking care of everyone else all the time—your children, the people at work, and your friends. And you've got to stop this. No you, no nothing. You must control yourself and it's not going to be easy.'"

This was not the first time Barbara had been warned to make her own life a priority. Auntie Abby reminded her again of an important lesson. Barbara has been a machinist, an actress, a journalist, a teacher, a therapist, a social activist, a community organizer, and the creator of numerous innovative projects and programs. Most recently, at Hewlett-Packard Labs, she organized a Creativity Day and co-created the exhibit called *Walk through Time* to invoke questions of world direction and corporate responsibility, which is now being published by John Wiley as a book. In addition, to demonstrate the controversial responses to an employee survey, she developed a "Reader's Theater" and had managers read the comments of secretaries, and vice versa, to improve communication and collaboration. Innovation comes naturally to her.

Since her encounter with Auntie Abby, Barbara has acknowledged that she is in the beginnings of a life transition. She's gone on a completely organic vegetarian diet. She is meditating, drawing,

And no one will listen to us until we listen to ourselves. The Goddess awakens in our hearts before she awakens in the world.
—MARIANNE WILLIAMSON, WRITER

writing, reading, and has spent an entire Saturday in solitude playing with ideas. Barbara has moved her personal development to the top of the list. This process will facilitate the emergence of creative insights to guide her into the next life phase, based on her personal needs.

Putting yourself at the top of your list means confronting the fear that if you do, someone else will lose out or be hurt. Joan L. Bolker, in her essay "A Room of One's Own Is Not Enough" from the book *The Writer's Home Companion,* states the truth very clearly when she writes, "One of the most important prerequisites of the creative process for a woman is the assurance that her work will not rupture the important connections of her life. Women are exquisitely sensitive to the possibility of such losses. And, while men are applauded for their creativity, women are often looked at askance, or asked if they've managed to write, or paint, or compose without harming someone else. We have to be quite tough to resist that sort of guilt. . . . But we ought not to have to choose between relationships and work, between caring for others and caring for ourselves, between the larger world and the self." Even today, there is a war of judgments between stay-at-home women and women in the workplace. Everyone has an opinion of the "right way" for women to behave and regardless of the choices we each make as individuals, someone is bound to disapprove. Our battle with the issue of caretaking versus creativity is too often waged with each other. The divide-and-conquer dynamic among women keeps too many women guilty, silent, and unexpressed. The whole point of the women's movement has been freedom of choice—a society that grants every woman the freedom to choose what's best for her as a unique individual.

All of the new feminist psychology studies have hailed women as relational beings whose top priority is relationship. It's certainly true for me. While I do not have children, my relationships, nevertheless, are the chosen focal point of my life. I wake up every morning and ponder other people's needs. My husband gets top priority as I "take his pulse" and try to tune into how I can support him that day. I often think about my clients in my early morning musings and get an idea for our next meeting. In my mind, I

> As for myself: I have flagrantly disobeyed the either-books-or-babes rule, having had three kids and written about twenty books, and thank God it wasn't the other way around.
> —URSULA K. LEGUIN, WRITER

scan my inner circle of family and friends, and my preference is to reach out and connect. Why do I do this? It's simply my core operating principle. But I have to be cautious as I am often guilty of self-forgetting. Being highly intuitive, I take in everyone else's agenda, which can eclipse my own. The creative act of writing this book has strengthened the development of my own self-focus. But it helped knowing that I wasn't writing this book just for me; I was writing it to inspire and empower women to break the cycle of intimidation and muteness.

Writing this book has taken years of serious intention and attention. I had to grant it top priority to sustain the commitment. It started out in this format, then became a novel, then became a book of twenty interviews, and finally returned to the original blueprint. All these delays and detours nourished the evolution of this book, but my major challenge was in reprogramming myself. In order to work on this book, I've had to resist a long to-do list of marketing projects, moneymaking opportunities, gardening, decorating, painting, housework, yardwork, organizing, partying, relaxing. I grew up in a tidy, organized family, so when there are unfinished projects all around me, like many women, I suffer from guilt. Coming from a heritage of domestic dynamos, with a grandmother who even ironed people's underwear, letting go of keeping everything neat and complete has been a test of inner strength. I had to resist the impossible expectations I set for myself in order to complete this work.

I've had to learn to walk by the weeds, blank out the peeling paint in the porch room, and live with closet chaos. My husband's unwavering emotional support combined with his willingness to handle the details of our lives has been essential to my success. So my struggle with self-focus has been an internal one. There was always a lot to pull me off track, and sometimes it took me a week to get back on the train, but I did. As a person with a constant flow of ideas and an unrealistic list of possible to-do's, I wrestled daily with narrowing the field.

Variety can be both seductive and destructive to our focus. Many creative women have more ideas than lifetimes; they continue to generate new ideas, but never complete their projects. I have a

> I don't wait for moods. You accomplish nothing if you do that. Your mind must know it has got to get down to earth.
> —PEARL S. BUCK, WRITER

client like that right now. She is simultaneously writing a screenplay, a book of poems, and newspaper articles, and continues to write new material in response to writing contests. Yet, nothing gets completed, as she's always adding more goals. We are working on her blocks to completion so that her screenplay gets sold.

A lovely book by Sue Bender, *Plain and Simple,* tells of her journey of discovery about the power of focus needed to write her book, beginning with a fascination for Amish quilts: "To my surprise, keeping my attention steady and confined to a few activities built a whole new discipline. A single-minded focus—repetition, order, an 'inspired monotony'—wasn't hateful and didn't limit me; the structure brought a different kind of freedom." Her life became integrated as one art form.

I have found Sue's wisdom to be true for me as well. Organizing my life around its priorities—relationships, creative work, and service—has a calming effect. Also, as I learned earlier when I was ill, people and activities that detract from my quality of life flash into my solitude like neon lights. Self-focus brings with it the gifts of clarity and higher standards.

Priorities also dictate our choices. I asked actress C. C. H. Pounder if she allows things like housework to get in the way of what she wants to do.

She was adamant: "No, I never let it. If there's something I want to see, like a play coming in from a foreign land for only two days, I'm going to the play. I might even have two or three guests come back to the house with me even if my beds aren't made and there are dishes in the sink. I'm not going to dash home and run around like a madwoman, washing and cleaning and setting everything up. I just tell people my bed's unmade and the dishes are in the sink, but I don't give up the play."

In Brenda Ueland's book *If You Want to Write,* there is a chapter called "Why women who do too much housework should neglect it for their writing." Brenda's insights hold true today: "In fact, that is why the lives of most women are so vaguely unsatisfactory. They are always doing secondary and menial things (that do not require all their gifts and ability) for *others* and never anything for *themselves.* Society and husbands praise them for it. . . .

> No one can give you authority. But if you act like you have it, others will believe you do.
> —Karin Ireland,
> writer

85

The poor wives are reminded that that is just why women are so splendid—because they are so unselfish and self-sacrificing and that is the wonderful thing about them! But inwardly women know that something is wrong. But after all these centuries of belief that women should be only encouragers and fosterers of talent in others, and have none of their own (as though you can effectively foster or encourage other people's talents unless you have a great deal of your own!) it is hard to do. I know that. But if women once learn to be something themselves, that the only way to teach is to be fine and shining examples, we will have in one generation the most remarkable and glorious children."

Judith Pierce Rosenberg has written a provocative book called *A Question of Balance: Artists and Writers on Motherhood.* In this book she profiles the determination and perseverance of creative women who work and parent simultaneously. The book talks about the need for mothers to find blocks of time to create and advises young women to establish their careers before they embark on having children. As so often is true in the arts, money for creative work appears later and in context, and a mother's challenge to value her work and balance that with the needs of children does demand a special approach. As Judith says in her introduction, "Like most of the women interviewed—who spoke with incredible honesty, but were, at the same time, concerned that their words might hurt a loved one—I find that I remain torn between the deep pull of work and the equally deep pull of family. And yet from the depths of this division, new work continues to emerge."

I asked Dr. Clarissa Pinkola Estés the question, "How have relationships and caring for others—mate, children, parents—impacted your work?" She replied, "Deeply. Without *mi familiares* I would know nothing." How does she juggle it all? "With *las agonistas* sometimes, in agony for my lost work. Keeping promises to my family of elders, children, and grandchildren is not a juggling act, but *the* priority."

Challenge: DISABLING DISTRACTIONS

Do you allow others to distract or interrupt you during your creative work time? Do you sabotage yourself by not turning

> Grab the broom of anger and drive off the beast of fear.
>
> —ZORA NEALE HURSTON, NOVELIST

off the phone or announcing to the people you live with that this is your designated creative time? Do you find yourself attending to other activities to avoid your creative work? What steps can you take to protect yourself from distractions or your own procrastination or sabotage?

Honoring Your Holistic Style

Not only have our daily roles and responsibilities been influenced by our cultural norms, but we must process these dilemmas in a linear world—yet another hurdle unique to women. As we know, men and women often think differently about things and have diverse communication styles—hence the focus these days on gender-speak. Many women think holistically, so, as women, our creative style sets us apart and makes for different challenges. In her book, *The Woman's Book of Creativity*, C. Diane Ealy writes about women's holistic process: "We see the whole first, then break out the details. Men tend to do the opposite. They use linear thinking, seeing the details first, then fit those together to form the whole. Linear thinking is what we learned in school as 'logical thinking.' We were told any other process was illogical and, therefore, no good. Holistic thinking is natural for most women, while linear thinking is natural for most men—although both sexes are certainly capable of using each type. Since Nature never creates waste, holistic and linear thinking exist to balance each other." In Western culture, linear thinking is revered and many of us as women learned to deny or depreciate our holistic thinking styles. No wonder low self-esteem and a tendency to devalue our problem-solving style is so prevalent in women (and men who think holistically as well). For too many women, doubting the legitimacy of their inspirations chokes their creative spirit.

Carol Frenier takes this concept one step further in her breakthrough book *Business and the Feminine Principle*. Carol compares the concepts of "diffuse awareness" and "focused consciousness" by saying, "Feminine diffuse awareness takes in everything. What you see is a field rather than a series of points, constantly seeing the complex relationships between things as an important piece of information in itself. Diffuse awareness does not edit." This information makes me chuckle because how many of us have been asked by the men in our lives to "hurry up and get to the point"? Our big picture view is a strength. For years I have heard clients and friends complain that their fathers/brothers/husbands/lovers miss the larger perspective and that their role as women is often to get the men to tune in.

Carol Frenier defines "focused consciousness" as a central quality of masculinity: "It means being able to separate and distinguish one thing from another, including one's own individuality from that of the group, and to be able to build something using information and ideas. As it separates one thing from another, focused consciousness has a natural tendency toward hierarchical ordering, because it sees the inherent qualities or lack thereof in each object. Such thinking has produced not only technologies for living, but philosophies, religions, and abstract thinking."

Creativity, like everything else, requires both diffuse awareness and focused consciousness. We need to harness our ability to scan and detect all the possible elements and then focus our attention laser-like on our specific project. My struggle and that of my female colleagues and clients is learning this focused consciousness with a starting place of self—hence "self-focus." In order to create, listen, honor our process, and follow where it leads, we must care for ourselves as a valuable conduit of ideas and actions. We must value our discoveries and then balance them with our caretaker pulls. As women, we are acutely aware of all the dynamics in our relationship circles. To accomplish our goals, we have to learn to redirect our senses from caretaking to creativity and that may not be our normal style. I had to let go of my domestic "shoulds" and put my work first to complete this book. I had to be less available to everyone else to serve the goddess of this book for a time. Therefore, I have had to master discipline and letting go.

Yet I need to add here that what's most important for you is accepting and validating your own style. For example, Marilyn Veltrop says, "I need to use both my right brain and my left brain. Yet, I can't allow my left brain to dominate and that's what it tends to like to do. So I have to let my intuition be the guide and the lead, and then it works. I feel the need to approach things using both my intuition and analytical mind. Until I come up with a way to honor both, I feel stuck and anxious. The narrative poem form that I'm using for the stories in my dissertation emerged for me naturally. It wasn't until several years later, after I started to use it, that I saw a similar form for the first time in Paula Underwood's book, *The Walking People,* an oral history of her Native ancestors. That was a lovely affirmation of it, and also a linking of it to Native roots, which are an important part of my heritage." For Marilyn, this poem form frees her creative energy and supports her ability to foster the writer in her. For each of us, claiming our own creative formula strengthens and expands our capabilities. If you allow patriarchal teachings to inhibit developing your own methodology, you've lost the battle.

Setting Boundaries

In all my years as a stress management consultant, I noticed that it was much more difficult for women than men to set boundaries in their lives. Women were much more likely to put up with being underpaid, overworked, unappreciated, and overextended in all areas of their lives. Burnout is frequently caused by not being able to say the simple word *No.* Yet setting strong personal boundaries is the way we protect ourselves as creative vessels, which is fundamental to creative work. You have to be able to dwell in your own private sphere to create. That's where the masculine strength of focused consciousness can assist us if we can leverage it; it helps us feel separate from everyone else and therefore legitimizes our self-focus.

As Sidra Stone reminds us, women need to acknowledge that our inner patriarch has some valuable lessons for us about boundaries. In *The Shadow King,* Sidra makes the following essential point: "The fourth lesson is one of focus and discipline. The Inner Patriarch knows all about focusing upon a piece of work that he wants to do and disciplining himself to resist distractions in order to finish it. He does not allow himself to be distracted by the needs or demands of others. What is important to him is his first priority.... If you, as a woman, resist his demands for you to give the men and the children in your life first priority, and you do your own work, you will not only be integrating his energies and using them consciously, but eventually you will earn his grudging respect and support."

Many of the women I interviewed for this project used strong tactics to set boundaries. "Deadlines invoke the fear of God in me," says career guide Barbara Sher. "A deadline gives me the right to sit down and create instead of cleaning house or doing my taxes. A deadline gives me permission to give those tasks to other people and pay them because I have to write this book. My publisher will be mad at me if I don't get my book done. And I screen all my calls and tell my friends that I can't go out and not to come over. I tell them that if they want to drop off some barley soup, leave it with the doorman—they can't come in. If I get scared enough about my deadline, I'll go somewhere to get away."

Artist and writer Cathleen Rountree puts a message on her answering machine saying that she is on "writing retreat" and might not call back for several weeks. Illustrator Jan Brett has help from her husband Joe in setting boundaries. He's "like a cop," protecting her from interruptions and those difficult "No"s: "Joe can say No to people and do it in a nice way so I don't look like a mean ogre. I don't generally divide things up into sexual roles. But as a female, one of the most difficult expectations of me is that I should do things for free, or sometimes not for free. There's this expectation that I should let my heart be the thing that makes me decide to do something rather than my right to make a decision based on whether or not I have enough time to do it." Jan also has two phone lines as another strategy to protect herself: "Nine times out of ten, I will not pick up the business line because it's generally somebody who wants me to do something I don't want to be talked into. But when my personal line rings, I know it's somebody in my family; that structure is very helpful to me." Hiring assistants to help you maximize your creative time is also another effective boundary-setting tool. For instance, in addition to Joe, Jan has an assistant. We only have so much energy, and hiring domestic or business help is a self-focus skill that preserves our best energy for our actual creative work. If you don't have the financial resources

> Fear of success can also be tied into the idea that success means someone else's loss. Some people are unconsciously guilty because they believe their victories are coming at the expense of another.
> —JOAN C. HARVEY, WRITER

to hire help, improvise. Envision what you want and experiment with trades, volunteers, interns. Be willing to proactively go after what you need.

Challenge: SUPPORT SYSTEMS

What support systems can you introduce into your life to ensure that the people you are responsible for are taken care of safely and appropriately while you utilize your high energy for your creative process?

Creating Solitude

Taking time to be totally alone is another important self-focusing technique. "At one point I had four books sitting on the shelf that had not gotten commercially published," said Lucia Capacchione. "So I just decided to put the steam on. From a big house in Pacific Palisades, I moved into a little ashram, a tiny room with a room-mate, with no domestic responsibilities whatsoever, except for *seva* (selfless service in the ashram), and I dedicated myself to editing those books into publishable form and getting them commercially distributed." Health spas, writers and artists retreat centers, and vacant summer/winter houses are all possible hideaways. The trick becomes giving yourself permission to indulge in the luxury of them.

Successful creative women also know the importance of self-care. Interior designer Chris Madden postponed our interview so she could sneak off to her favorite spa in Connecticut for a few days as she'd been working nonstop for too long a stretch. She also wrote part of her latest book on retreat there.

"Quality attention is the greatest gift we have to give to others and ourselves," says attention expert Alice Aspen March. For her-self, Alice realized that her personal creative longings demanded *her* full attention. She realized that she could not write at home because she felt constantly interrupted. After coping with the scare of a surgical breast biopsy, she made an overnight decision to take off to Maui to see if she could realize her dream of writing about the vital role that attention plays in our lives. Her husband balked, several women urged her to stay closer to home, but she went anyway and immersed herself totally in her own process for two weeks.

Alice's creativity flowered and flowed. She learned that she needed warmth, visual beauty, physical space, solitude, and uninterrupted time to write how she wanted to. She decided that she was writing as a mentor to women, and simultaneously started a children's book. I asked Alice what made this trip work so well for her, and she said, "This was really the first time I ever gave myself permission to create the time and space I always knew I needed— to do nothing except write for as long as I wanted, even through dinner. I got to experience what I had always intuitively sensed I needed, but which my caretaking self had always deprived me of."

As Gail Jones, owner of A Mother's Place, which offers transition groups for mothers in Topsfield, Massachusetts, says, "Solitude is mandatory for staying connected to one's own soul." Since creativity comes from our soul, we need quiet time to connect with the soul's messages. Creative thoughts percolate in silence, in an atmosphere where we can escape the noise and the needs of others. We must dialogue with ourselves and then review the content. We must be still enough to listen and cultivate our creative impulses. Successful creative women value their time enough not to be seduced into doing things that they don't really want to do—unless they choose to. In order to succeed, you must create a space, commit the time, value it, and fight for it. And yes, give some things up. The states of solitude and caretaking, including parenting, oppose each other. Sorting out our values and priorities entails a very personal journey for every woman.

Supporting Self-Focus in Other Women

The issues around creativity versus caretaking have long polarized women against each other. We each need to live by our own truths and values. The challenge for many of us is transcendence of other people's expectations and making peace with our own choices and priorities. That's why we also need to monitor our tendency to pass

> Only when one is connected to one's inner core is one connected to others. And, for me, the core, the inner spring, can best be re-found through solitude.
>
> —ANNE MORROW LINDBERGH, WRITER

judgment on other women for their similarly difficult choices. Whenever you find yourself criticizing another woman for her life choices, stop for a moment. Do you really know what obstacles she faces in her life? Are you sure you have the right formula for everyone? Monitor your judgments of other women and notice what you observe. Attacking each other doesn't solve the problems we all face as modern women. Let's try to focus on the big picture of the challenges that women face today as they try to manage multiple worlds of expectations. It is important that we stop splitting ourselves off from one another and band together to create new freedoms and support systems for ourselves and the next generations of women. By cultivating our own self-focus and encouraging that of our peers, we can harness even more creative power in the world.

Challenge: RELEASING JUDGMENTS AND SUPPORTING OTHER WOMEN

What judgments do you hold about other women and their choices around being creative? Are there any judgments you can release? Think of other women you know that you could support by offering to help them commit to their creativity. Could you baby-sit for them, attend classes with them, or simply talk with them about their work and their goals? You will learn more about yourself in the process.

Conquering Saboteurs

In order to leverage your creative growth, you need to defend yourself from saboteurs, both internal and external.

- Valuing Your Natural Abilities
- Faking It Until You Make It
- Transcending Your Wounds
- Overcoming the Fear of Criticism
- Dealing with the Fear of Too Much
- Recognizing Real Saboteurs
- Cultivating Self-Defense

When the Diary came out and I heard from many women,
I heard about their timidities, their lack of confidence,
their reliance upon others. If someone criticized their work,
for example, they would almost fall apart. Then I
remembered my own vulnerabilities and my own
hesitancies and my own timidities, and I wanted
you to know that they can be overcome.

—ANÄIS NIN, WOMEN, CREATIVITY, AND THE ARTS

*I*n coaching, we call these vulnerabilities that Nin is talking about "gremlins"—those persistent little voices of doubt and fear that eclipse our aspirations and self-confidence. Unconscious or unmanaged gremlins can subvert, wreck, undermine, or destroy our great inspirations. For creative women, self-sabotage poses a serious risk to the completion of work. To become a woman who expresses her creativity, as opposed to a woman who just dreams about it, mastering these nasty gremlins becomes an essential competence.

It's hard to say which gremlins are more damaging: the taunting of self-doubts or the external voices from society—parents, teachers, or other authority figures.

Add to the mix the traumatizers who become our ghosts from the past condemning us for self-expression, and we have the potential for great suppression. Many of the women I interviewed had horror stories to tell about humiliation, yet it is hopeful to know that their creative passions transcended the wounds. They reassure us that we can take charge of our gremlins.

Self-doubt looms ominously for women. Creative people often work outside a supportive structure, so maintaining confidence in ourselves and our work requires vigilance. In writing this chapter, I once again confronted my own self-doubt. The process recalled what happened years ago when I wrote and produced my audiotape. During the process of writing the script, managing a difficult producer, and fielding all of the unknowns, I had a blind confidence that all of it would work out. But when I picked up the completed shrink-wrapped copies at the post office, I got into a minor car accident on the way home. Surprisingly, seeing my dream project in tangible form both startled and scared me. It looked too good.

Similarly, when Conari Press expressed strong interest in this book after years of my own dedication to it, suddenly, for a few days, I decided it was "too hard" and lost all motivation. Yet, writing this book has been sacred work for me; stopping had never been an option. So why did I decide suddenly that I didn't want to do it? Fear, of course. Fear that I didn't have anything original to say, and that everyone who read the book would be critical of it.

Also, it's been unnerving that, during the writing of this book, I've had relentless technical difficulties with tape recorders and computers. Coincidence? Maybe, but certainly still exasperating challenges. I've had to don my warrior persona repeatedly.

When I think about it, though, if I'm successful, whom will I hurt? No one in my inner circle that I can think of. I'm not afraid of outdoing my loved ones—my mother sends me articles on creative women all the time; my father scored a couple of people for me to interview at a cocktail party; and one of my brothers got me in touch with the owners of Vera Bradley. My husband understands how important this book is to me and has willingly made sacrifices in support of it. But there's a psychic level of apprehension. Like some of the women I've interviewed, I've always sensed the presence of an unconscious deep awareness of the danger of true self-expression for women. After all, our female ancestors were burned and murdered for their intuitive, creative, and healing powers. I do believe that we women have a shared legacy of anxiety about becoming too influential and then being attacked. As Naomi Wolf says in her important book, *Fire with Fire,* "In women, powerlessness has been sexy for a long time."

One of the most tragic stories of self-doubt and self-destruction came from Cathleen Rountree. She brought the slides of her Demon Series paintings to our interview, which vividly portray the story of her childhood sexual abuse. In her late twenties, images came to her through her dreams, and she spontaneously painted a series of larger-than-life pieces about her demons. Step by step, she portrayed the images of her persecution and her inner turmoil in visible form. Unable to handle the intensity of what she had

> Our deepest fear is not that we are inadequate. Our deep fear is that we are powerful beyond measure.
> —MARIANNE WILLIAMSON, WRITER

created, Cathleen believed that if she destroyed the paintings that she would be free of her pain. After photographing the paintings, she and a friend took the huge original paintings by truck into a forest, and destroyed them one at a time.

She had hoped this ritual would bring relief to her psyche, but she now knows that it was fear that propelled her to destroy this museum-quality collection of art.

Following the destruction of her artwork, Cathleen catapulted into a depression and went into a long retreat for many weeks. Writing helped her to reconnect with her soul. In her work, Cathleen explores her inner questions and has healed herself and many others. I was so honored that she shared the slides of these Demon paintings with me. The images on the slides are startling but depict the terror and betrayal she experienced. Yet her final painting portrays freedom and recovery. When she is ready, I do hope that Cathleen will either exhibit or publish these images—they are truly astounding. As Cathleen experienced, fear as a saboteur can become the great destroyer—be careful of its tricks.

Challenge: YOUR PERSONAL SABOTEURS

Identify your personal saboteurs and their specific messages to you. Name the different voices inside of you: the pusher, the slugger, the critic. Make a list of all of the humiliating experiences in your life or times that you felt shamed. Consider how these experiences may be thwarting your creative expression now.

Valuing Your Natural Abilities

Women have long had the self-destructive habit of discounting themselves and their natural abilities. C. Diane Ealy, author of *The Women's Book of Creativity* and co-author of *Our Money, Ourselves: A Guide to Redesigning Your Relationship with Money,* discounted her ability to write because it came so naturally. This is a common gremlin, assuming that what comes easily to us is not

> You gain strength, courage and confidence by every experience in which you really stop to look fear in the face. You are able to say to yourself, "I lived through this horror. I can take the next thing that comes along." You must do the thing you think you cannot do.
>
> —ELEANOR ROOSEVELT, ACTIVIST

valuable or unique. As Diane says, "I wrote a lot of poetry when I was a kid—which I did not show to anybody. I kept it really private. But I also had this mindset—I think it's fairly typical of women—that I did not appreciate the talent that I had. I can remember friends calling me to help them when they were stuck on a writing assignment. On the phone, I'd say, 'Well, why don't you try this' and then I'd dictate a few sentences. It didn't yet register that I had an ability." It took Diane several decades to finally claim the writer in her, and she struggled through multiple rewrites and roadblocks to produce her first book. Outsmarting those doubting voices by achieving our goals gives us more access to a stronger self and more resilience to draw on in the future.

Ginny O'Brien, author of *Fast Forward M.B.A.* and *Success on Her Own Terms: Tales of Extraordinary, Ordinary Women,* and an accomplished chef who had also made her daughter an astonishingly beautiful handpainted bedroom set, initially wondered why I was interviewing her as a creative woman. She didn't see herself as outstanding enough to be written about. It's all part of our training to push others into the limelight and be a support person rather than a rainmaker ourselves. Ginny's creativity is multifaceted and obvious to anyone who meets her. When you visit her home, signs of Ginny's artistry beckon you from everywhere, from the meditation corner and floral design of her garden to her own framed drawings on the walls.

As a young wife, Ginny taught herself to cook by reading cookbooks. For her, cooking expresses her love of the visual. "I see cooking as very creative," she remarked. "I think the creativity comes from the presentation, as well as having the food taste good. We always sit down with placemats and napkins so the table looks beautiful. I love giving dinner parties where we wind up just sitting around the table having conversation. But every process of making a nice meal has a spiritual element in it; it's giving food and nourishment. It's a sacred way to provide for someone. So in my life, even when my first husband left, my daughter and I always sat down to dinner and I prepared nice food, just for the two of us. It became a ritual."

Another ritual, this one in the morning, helped Ginny create her two books and a new direction for herself as a coach. In the early 1990s, "I started reading about imaging," she recalls, "and how you could control your future by visualizing what you want. I'm very disciplined and I created a vision about my writing a book and all the steps. There was a chapel downstairs from my office at that time and I never went to work without first stopping in the chapel and meditating on my vision. I'd actually like to write a book called *Prayer Works* because I definitely think my two books came about because of that." Ginny now continues her visioning in her living room armchair. For many women who have experienced lack of encouragement or trauma in their life experiences, prayer and visualization can be powerful antidotes to those harassing voices of self-doubt. These spiritual practices overpower a lack of confidence and cement a vision of expanded possibilities. For too many women, limited thinking holds them back. Visualizing what you want on a daily basis prepares you to manifest it.

Faking It Until You Make It

To fear is one thing. To let fear grab you by the tail and swing you around is another.
—Katherine Paterson, writer

Along with visualizing results, we have to connect with our inner power. For twice Emmy-award nominated actress C. C. H. Pounder, the challenge of a new role stirs the cauldron of fear for her. She told me a great story of this process, complete with all the dramatic intonations of her unforgettable trained voice: "What makes me nervous is when I finally get an opportunity to play a new role; there's this moment of feeling absolutely petrified because I've never played it before. I got a great chance with Mike Nichols to play Meryl Streep's psychiatrist in the film Postcards from the Edge. I was incredibly excited but I went to the first reading and I became this quiet little person and Mike said, 'I know you can do this. What are you doing?' I told him, 'I panicked but I'll get over it.' I had to convince myself that the same attitude I have in real life at the bank or when someone sends me a bill that's wrong is what's required for this. It's not that I haven't been an authority in life. So I became myself and acted as I do when I know I'm in the right and then transferred it back to this psychiatrist and got the part. Of course then I got six doctor roles in a row and plunged into the medical profession as an actress." From her insights about acting, C. C. H. knows the value of communication with both self and the audience, and the power of projection. Her story reminds me of the old axiom "Fake it until you make it," which as creative women we often need to remember to help us conquer the next hurdle.

Transcending Your Wounds

In Janet Hagberg's enlivening book, *Wrestling with Angels: A Spiritual Journey to Great Writing,* she calls great writing "soul writing." Interestingly, she believes that wrestling with the angel who holds the key to our brilliance is often more challenging than embracing the critic. She says, "Wrestling with our angel involves three central themes that relate directly to the intimacy and the spirituality of the writing process: discovering how our shadow blocks our writing, experiencing the gift of great and courageous writing, and giving writing a sacred place in our lives. When we begin wrestling with our angels, we discover our own dark shadows, the hidden parts of ourselves that sabotage us and hinder our writing process. We understand how our own woundedness is a step in our journey to wholeness."

Janet and I talked about how her words ring true for all creative journeys. By owning our wounds, we can move beyond them. When her own demons show up, Janet goes for a walk because, as she says, "My demons don't like fresh air." Janet has gotten to know one of her demons, the one she calls Rude, intimately. As Janet says, "He's an old, gruff-looking, long-bearded Scandinavian type. He's the mythology for my upbringing. He exudes that stern never-be-vulnerable-always-be-strong and never-let-anybody-know-that-you're-a-human-being persona. He's a tough-guy Viking. When he bothers me, I send him to clean files. I also bump into a lot of Rudes out there in the world, and he helps me understand that they may be rude on the outside but they're little kids on the inside who need a lot of love and support. So I'm less afraid of being afraid as I learn how to deal with them."

Therapy, women's support groups, and other self-awareness ventures all help us detach from any internal sabotage system we're plugged into. If you feel overwhelmed and helpless in the wake of your self-doubt, get some support to break the cycle. You have brilliance; you can let it emanate.

Challenge: HEALING OLD WOUNDS

What messages did you receive as a child, a young woman, or an adult about the dangers of becoming a successful creative woman?

Which of those messages do you believe and which ones can you now discard? Determine if your gremlin voices have any wisdom to share with you as perhaps they protect you in some way. Instruct them how they might best be helpful to you now. If their messages seem to have no merit at the moment, close your eyes and envision your gremlins banished to Antarctica.

Overcoming the Fear of Criticism

In *Fire with Fire,* Naomi Wolf writes about two specific internal saboteur voices that torment many women: "When I was twenty-six, my first book, *The Beauty Myth,* was published. Soon after, I was set upon by my own dragons. The ones that nailed me are familiar to many women: The dragon of the Fear of Criticism and the dragon of the Fear of Having Too Much. Witnessing my own ambivalence about attaining a measure of power led me to look around and realize, first, that I had a great deal of company; and second, that no legislative or professional victory will bring women full equality—or happiness—if they fail to develop a new psychology of power."

This vulnerability to the judgments of others was mentioned often by the women I interviewed. Ceramist Rosette Gault cleverly engineered the introduction of her paper clay step by step. She even had special photographs prepared to convince the more left-brain skeptics that her invention was scientifically solid. She silenced her

> Some of us just go along . . . until that marvelous day people stop intimidating us—or should I say we refuse to let them intimidate us?
> —PEGGY LEE,
> SINGER

critics one by one by preparing herself in advance for their objections. She anticipated potential criticisms or skepticism and had an answer for each possibility.

Hers is a true victory, and one for each of us to make note of. When you introduce a creative idea or product, someone will throw darts at you, so steel yourself ahead of time and plan your defense: Who will object and why? Who is threatened by the change or the advance you are proposing? Who may just want to undermine you for some reason? Ask yourself all the vicious questions you can think of that someone may use to attack you, and then ask your peers to add to the list.

Even more daring an action is to find someone whom you know has a totally opposite thinking style or set of values than you and solicit their comments. This exercise may be unnerving, but it will help you stay centered, confident in your own creative connections, and prepared for controversy. When we put ourselves out there, we open ourselves up to possible attack. We have to defend ourselves, make sound decisions, and hold our stance. That's why so many creative women talk about the importance of using rituals to stay grounded to the earth and spirit. Like a strong tree trunk rooted in the earth, the winds of criticism won't knock us over as easily if we have a solid base.

Like most women, I battle the Fear of Criticism dragon. Having grown up in a perfectionist family, being exposed for making a mistake still has the potential to unglue me. With the benefits of therapy and middle age, I now accept that mistakes are inevitable and generally not life threatening. Recently, I transformed two brand new lampshades that I accidentally ruined with scissors into originals by gluing silk flowers over the gaping holes. Instead of shame, I felt the euphoria of creative conquest, for my new lampshades look smashing. With my writing, I have enlisted a group of wise and candid editors for support and welcome their comments. But I know that there are critics in my future and that my warrior instincts will be challenged to fight the dragon.

> As the feminine spirit seeks to rise, there are numerous forces seeking to push her back down.
> —MARIANNE WILLIAMSON, WRITER

Dealing with the Fear of Too Much

For designer Joanne Rossman, the dragon of the Fear of Too Much is often hot on her tail. While she's very abundant in her life on many levels, she has dealt with the chronic business problem of lack of capital: "Money's a real challenge. Yet the amazing thing is that I live like I have lots of money. My life has had that kind of charm. I think somewhere inside, in some little corner of me, I'm still poor."

Joanne loves to travel, joyfully embraces the adventures of living, and surrounds herself with aesthetic pleasures. Her house was recently featured in the *Boston Globe,* and her studio doubles as an antique gallery. Her pattern has been to spend all the money that comes in and "live on the edge." Accumulating dollars has not yet been comfortable, though she is now beginning to invest for retirement. As Joanne admits, she has a voice inside of her that calls her a fraud, based on her insecurity about not having a degree: "There's a strong voice inside of me that says, 'Who do you think you are? And how can you possibly make money? How is it you've fooled all these people all this time with your work?'"

This fear that we ought to have all kinds of credentials to truly earn our success raises havoc with our faith in our work. Having money and success often requires some internal rewiring. C. Diane Ealy's new book on money exudes her strong beliefs about this internal dispute. As Diane told me, "The final frontier for evolving women involves facing and resolving our money issues. Once we clear out our negative messages, we are free to reconceptualize and redefine money, embracing its spiritual aspects. Money then becomes a partner on our journey toward expressing our unique creative selves."

Recognizing Real Saboteurs

Parents, teachers, and competitors can fuel our gremlins and short-circuit our creative unfolding. Maureen Murdock knew she wanted to be a visual artist before age five, but her father's attitude discouraged her: "My father was a visual artist who could replicate anything he saw. I remember longing to be able to draw what I saw in nature two-dimensionally. One day I was sitting in the basement looking up through one of those transom windows at a tree. I said, 'Dad, teach me to draw a tree.' He said, 'Well, look at the tree and then draw it.' And I said, 'No, I want you to teach me how.' And that's when he said that you either have talent or you don't. When you get that message at age five, it's hard to overcome."

Marcia Yudkin, author of nine books and an upcoming PBS program on amateur musicians, and a keynote speaker at writers' conferences, had an experience with an "expert" that could have blocked her creative expression: "After I had been writing seriously for a year, I went to a famous writers' conference where a well-known writer tore my work apart in a very destructive way in front of a hundred people. I was devastated. I can imagine that a lot of people would have stopped writing after an experience like that, but the criticism was confusing. Maybe that's what helped me bounce back from it. He didn't explain what was wrong with my writing in a way that I could understand. He just gave these pronouncements, you shouldn't do this, this, and this, but he never explained why. On the other hand, if he'd been able to communicate it in a way that made sense I might have been able to glean something from it. I didn't learn anything except not to go to that writers' conference."

Illustrator Jan Brett has been remarkably successful, but academic gremlins are uncomfortable for her at times. She knew as a child that she had talent and would become an illustrator, yet she didn't follow an academic track: "I'll get frustrated because there's a big valley between schools of thought. It's not so much male/female for me—it's academic versus creative. Critics, academic people, and librarians want to categorize things and have them set up in a way for people to learn. Whereas my viewpoint is more, I like to create. And boy, isn't it nice that kids like my books. Hey, that's great. I'm often asked questions that someone would ask an expert in education or children's literature—but that's not what I do. I just draw pictures. So that's a frustration. Lots of times artwork is judged in an academic way rather than whether it works as a piece of art or literature. It's an experience and people have different reactions. If it's working, then who cares what theory it fits into?"

> Creative minds have always been known to survive any kind of bad training.
> —Anna Freud, analyst

For so many young women for whom creativity is not nurtured at home, school has the potential to be a golden opportunity. Not so for career expert Barbara Sher. She told me about two encounters with teachers that sabotaged her self-expression: "I never knew anybody creative in school. I didn't know one writer or one artist, but I tried writing for the junior high newspaper. My sewing teacher, a strict teacher, told me she liked one of the columns I wrote. So, I wrote another and then she told me she was disappointed in me. She told me it wasn't as good as the last one, but I didn't know what she was talking about. I just could never write again. I was devastated. I think she wanted me to learn to write better, but I couldn't handle the criticism."

Later in college, another teacher eclipsed her love affair with the camera: "I took up photography as I had a natural ability. I got into a few shows and I did some nice pieces. My photography teacher was a very pleasant guy but he said, 'Look, you really have a good eye but your negatives look like a truck drove over them. I want you to get some good film and change your whole gray range.' So I bought some quality film, set up these statues, and tried to take pictures. Then he said, 'Forget everything I told you. I feel like I ruined all your spontaneity.' It was true—I didn't want to take any more pictures.... I felt like I lost my eye."

Barbara spoke out very strongly about the power of misguided teachers who become internalized as gremlins: "A good teacher is the holiest of God's creatures. I don't think that there's another role in our culture that deserves the rank of holy except a great teacher who excites you. And the bad teachers should be made to march in chains. I don't care if you're just teaching someone to play the guitar or how to fix a car. When people love to learn and they feel it's safe to try things with someone to help them along, that's great. Anybody who stops that has murder on their souls; they've got blood on their hands."

So often, teachers don't even realize that their admonishments and criticisms rob a child of the courage to be original and take risks with her ideas. Almost everyone I talked with recalled such an episode. Designer Joanne Rossman told this story: "I remember in the seventh grade, I took a sewing class and I failed it. I had taken

> I went for years not finishing anything. Because, of course, when you finish something you can be judged.... I had poems which were rewritten so many times I suspect it was just a way of avoiding sending them out.
> —ERICA JONG,
> WRITER

a pot holder home to hand-quilt it, not knowing you weren't supposed to do that, and so I got an F for the course. And you know, divine justice.... Years later, in 1970, I had a show in a gallery in my hometown in Nevada. Simultaneously, I gave a lecture at the University of Nevada and 250 people came, and one of them was my old sewing teacher. Now she probably doesn't recall giving me an F, but I certainly remembered it. I hated sewing as a result of that for many years."

Fortunately for Joanne, when her children were young, the wonderful clothes she wanted to buy them were expensive, so she started sewing again. Daring to defy that misguided teacher set Joanne on a professional track as a successful designer and seamstress. Her work is unusual and dramatic.

I, too, had an art teacher, accomplished enough to do courtroom drawings on television and portraits of my brother and me, who killed my interest in art early on. Once I made a ceramic ashtray for my mother for Mother's Day and my teacher's comment was, "You're not actually going to give her that, are you?" It took me until my thirties to dare to try any form of art again.

Parents and teachers are supposed to help, but often their own unresolved shames dictate their response to an innovation. Saboteurs are potentially everywhere. What's different about the women profiled in this book is that they transcended those voices of criticism, humiliation, and sometimes cruelty. Mastering the fear and proceeding in spite of it is the best revenge against society's thrust to keep women voiceless.

Challenge: RETAINING YOUR CREATIVE POWER

Write down a list of the times when you devalued or gave away your creative power. How can you prevent that from happening again? What support systems can help you to change that pattern? Are you aware of any fear of success for yourself? Dissect its components and strategize a plan to heal it.

People call me a feminist whenever I express sentiments that distinguish me from a doormat.
—REBECCA WEST, WRITER

Cultivating Self-Defense

Artist Carmella Yager has some excellent advice about the necessity of using discrimination when we handle criticism and negativity: "I think it's important to become deeply rooted in who you are, so that when you hear what other people say about your work, you are really listening, not just being defensive. Then you can go home and you can say, that was a mismatch, or I can let that comment roll off my back or that really hurt or gosh, they're right." We can listen to everything we hear, but then it's important to sort it out realistically, learn what we need to, and discard the rest. Not everyone is going to understand what we're up to. A critical skill for many creative women is discernment—knowing whose advice is from the heart and really meant to be helpful, and avoiding folks who pull you away from your intentions and may be trying to undermine your achievement.

Challenge: SELF-PROTECTION

What rituals or centering exercises can you do before you start your creative work to ward off your saboteurs? Begin today. Of all the proactive strategies used to ward off fear that you read about in this chapter, which ones resonated for you? Pick one or more, try them out yourself, and incorporate them into your repertoire.

SECRET 7

Consulting with Guides

As the creative path can be lonely and fraught with arduous challenges, help from guides can keep you centered and well-advised.

- Reading about Inspiring Lives
- Remembering Early Influences
- Seeking Out Role Models and Advisors
- Initiating or Joining a Group
- Guiding Others

*Over the decades, in the main, an inner force has infused
my work. It is a "Source without source" that has acted as a
cross-wind countering the more mundane winds of "no time, no
energy, flat-out exhausted." There have been a handful of loyal
and insightful souls—most never having graduated from grade-
school—who have stepped into my woods for brief periods of
time during this last fifty-two years. Even though "my work in
the cave" is, of necessity, deeply solitary, they have left little
trails of evanescent materials, such as bread crumbs, to momen-
tarily mark the path, or left some little twigs as tinder for
rekindling the fire, and an occasional cloak that when
donned, causes one to be able, temporarily, to fly.*

—Clarissa Pinkola Estés, *Born Awake*

There is a myth that in order to be creative you have to grow up in an avant-garde, artsy, liberal, permissive family, and experience extraordinary cultural exposure, travel, numerous lessons and educational opportunities, as well as receive constant adoration for your creative gifts. There's no question that a creative family can facilitate experimentation and self-confidence, but it's not mandatory. Many creative women, like many of the women profiled in this book, did not grow up in such enlightened, creative families. Regardless of your upbringing, you always have the option in adulthood to seek out guides on your own.

Attracting the right guides facilitates the ease of your creative journey. A guide is someone who sees who you are and helps you to find your way. Guides can be teachers, parents, relatives, mentors, psychotherapists, coaches, astrologists, psychics, shamans, friends, colleagues, organizations, communities, support groups, spiritual teachings, works of art, plays, movies, books, radio and television broadcasts, Internet information or chat sessions, or any other encounters with wisdom. The name of my first business, Guided Growth, came to me many years ago in a meditation. I have been a guide to many clients for twenty-five years and have sought out guidance for myself in many forms. Many of the women in this book have served as guides to other women and girls of all ages and their participation in this book is another installment of their willingness to share their insights.

A positive guide is someone who connects with your true self. Designer Diane Ericson shared two important encounters with people who truly understood her. She recalls that two weeks after her husband left her, she started teaching a course in fashion merchandising, which she'd never taught before, and was commuting to work thirty miles a day in an unreliable car, with a two-year-old in day care all day and a five-year-old in kindergarten. "By the time Christmas vacation rolled around, I considered committing suicide. I was doing the best I could and it wasn't really working. I'd never felt that way in my entire life. So I told this older friend of mine who's in her seventies now that I was thinking of not being around and she said, 'Geez—I'm surprised you didn't feel that way sooner.' I was relieved to know that it was okay to have that feeling, and I kept going!"

Another influential person in Diane's life has been Bill Veltrop, who is married to Marilyn Veltrop. In fact, Diane designed their sacred wedding attire.

Diane met Bill many years earlier at an EST personal development workshop and said that he was one of the few people she has ever met who could really listen to her. "Bill gave me this gift of listening to me without being overwhelmed, critical, or judging. After several hours, Bill said, and I will never forget this, because this was pivotal for me: 'You know, most people are trying to figure out how to build a launch pad. You're in outer space. You just have to figure out how to work the controls.' Thanks to Bill I was able to get into the driver's seat and steer so I could drive my energy where I wanted it to go, instead of being dragged along by it." It's amazing how the power of being heard and valued can clear the cobwebs and allow us to identify what we really want.

Sometimes guides are catalysts to our next step. Creativity consultant Donna Luther still corresponds with a college professor whom she met as a freshman and who directed her first college dramatic show. "He was always instrumental in helping me understand that I could do anything I wanted to do." He was the one who encouraged her to go to the Creative Problem-Solving

> Surround yourself with people who are going to lift you higher.
> —OPRAH WINFREY, TALK SHOW HOST AND ACTRESS

Institute Creativity Conference in Buffalo, New York, and participate for the first time. That advice changed Donna's life and sparked a national workshop business for her, as well as providing her with colleagues and new contacts. One of her workshop coleaders is a man who also believes in her talent. As Donna says, "He's one of those people who will stop me dead in my tracks and make me think about what decision I'm making. He has big ideas for me." Donna feels strongly that she wants to take things step by step but appreciates being encouraged.

Not all so-called guides are committed to our individuality. Some false guides seek our total allegiance and therefore fail us in the end. As originality is essential to the creative process, we need guides who can both nurture and then let go at the right time. A wise guide knows that the time will come when we will outgrow them or need additional voices. Exposure to many kinds of guides broadens our learning base and gives us more ideas from which to formulate our own creative stance.

Reading about Inspiring Lives

For many artists, writers, and self-employed women, guides are symbolic rather than real. Writer Ginny O'Brien says she has never had a mentor but was inspired by the writings of both Jean Baker Miller and Gail Sheehy. As Joan Jeruchim and Pat Shapiro write in *Women, Mentors, and Success,* "Women who work alone, such as writers and artists, often have a different problem in developing a professional identity. They work in an isolated setting and must create their own culture. Often they develop professional identities by studying others' works and fantasizing about symbolic mentors or role models. While it is difficult to maintain a personal relationship with a more established writer or artist, the careers of these symbolic mentors can be inspirational."

Reading provided Awiakta with a vision for her future as well. As she says, "I wanted to be a poet and a writer and I really wanted a family too. But in the early 1950s, when I was a teenager, I didn't know of any women writers with that combination. So after reading Eve Curie's biography of her mother, I chose physicist Marie

Curie as my role model. She was tenacious, brilliant, and intrepid. With her husband and colleague, Pierre, she created a stable family *and* discovered radium, for which they were awarded the Nobel Prize. Surely I could have a family and manage to do good work also." Her clarity guided her to the right husband and the richness of living she yearned for in both arenas.

Dancer Leslie Neal feels fortunate that so many of the pioneers in the field of dance were women who served as mentors-at-a-distance during her years of dance training. She cites two women in particular: "Some of Martha Graham's works and her words have been a constant source of inspiration. Isadora Duncan is the ultimate mentor for many of us because of her conviction, her strength, and her courage to combat so many of the social barriers of her time." But Leslie also found some of the histories about these dancers to be counterproductive: "As a young dancer growing up and reading about women choreographers and dancers, the focus was on all the many wonderful creative successful things they did without mentioning the hard challenging periods. So when I would face difficulties, I'd think, well, I must be doing something wrong, because they seem to just wake up in the morning, go to the studio, and get hit by divine inspiration every time. Yet now that some of them have published their memoirs or autobiographies, these great artists have revealed that they too had dark periods and that there are great hardships at times in creating work. That, on some strange level, was very comforting to me." The real story is so often much more helpful than a myth.

Remembering Early Influences

To connect to your creativity, it is important to think back to your childhood and recall who served as a role model. Writer Marcia Yudkin's tale of starting a family newspaper when she was eight depicts family backing. Marcia came up with the idea and began interviewing: "I asked my mother what each family member did and she gave me all of the family news. I wrote it up and added little cartoons, brainteasers, and people's birthdays and sent it out to both sides of the family." Her sister helped her to type it while her mother, a teacher, ran it off on the mimeo machine at school. But for Marcia, what was most exciting was when her uncle, who was in the newspaper business, got genuine newsprint cut to size for her project and sent her a big supply. So Marcia, who has since published many articles and books, experienced the thrill of being published early on. Marcia also read her poems on television before the age of seven, which is interesting as she is now doing radio commentaries and developing a television series.

Artist and writer Lucia Capacchione grew up in a creative Hollywood family. Her father was a film editor at MGM, working on films with stars such as Judy Garland, Fred Astaire, and Gene Kelly. Later he edited television classics such as *The Lone Ranger, Wild, Wild West,* and *The Brady Bunch.* Her dad let her accompany him on some of these adventures: "My dad would bring me to the editing room or onto the sets where I got to see them shooting movies. So I had a really close look at incredible talent and met people like Clark Gable when I was only eight years old." Lucia's mother was a dressmaker working with MGM as well as Beverly Hills designers, and Lucia lived with the excitement of her mother's home-based business. Specializing in weddings, her grandmother was also a successful dressmaker, so Lucia had two role models of "designing women." As an only child, Lucia grew up very much involved in her parents' work and their lives. I asked Lucia how all this glamour and creativity affected her life goals and she replied, "I always knew in my heart that I was going to have a career. I was really groomed for that. I was given art lessons when I wanted them or music lessons when I was ready. Any talent that showed up was nurtured. I was allowed to give plays in the backyard during the summer with my friends and invite the neighbors."

Chef Lydia Shire clearly says that she attributes much of her success to her parents, who she says were "people of great quality." Her parents were fashion and book illustrators in the style of Norman Rockwell. Lydia says her mother taught her all about color, and both of Lydia's restaurants are uniquely dramatic in their use of different hues. Her love of cooking came from her father, of whom Lydia says, "My father was a great cook—even though he was Irish. He used to have me chop garlic with a big cleaver for spaghetti aioli when I was four years old."

> If a child is to keep alive his inborn sense of wonder, he needs the companionship of at least one adult who can share it, rediscovering with him the joy, excitement, and mystery of the world we live in.
> —RACHEL CARSON, BIOLOGIST AND WRITER

Designer Sigrid Olsen also grew up in an artistic family. Her dad was an artist, her mother was artistic, and they lived in a community of artists in Connecticut. Sigrid remembers that she began drawing as soon as she could hold a pencil or a crayon: "As a child, I drew to entertain myself, and a lot of the drawing I did was very decorative, with patterns on the edge of ladies' skirts and so forth, so it's ironic that now I'm in the business of using that decorative kind of artwork."

Photographer Alison Shaw's mother was a professional photographer before she focused on raising her children. So Alison had access to a set-up darkroom and was taking pictures at a very young age, although she was more attracted to painting at first. She also acknowledges that she grew up in a creative context: "The whole environment I grew up in was very nurturing for my creativity. There was never any pressure that I should be doing things any other way. My parents never tried to take control over my interests or directions."

Innovation expert Pam Moore says she always felt creative and describes her parents as "incredibly resourceful, creative, and improvisational." She says that as a child she didn't realize that they didn't have very much money because she was raised in an atmosphere of plenty: "My parents are both incredibly gifted and talented in being able to take whatever materials are available and use them. My dad can build all kinds of things with his hands. My mom paints, sews, and upholsters. She'll attack anything; she is fearless in that. So both of them were my models."

Author Shakti Gawain also credits her mother for teaching her about possibilities: "I come from quite a long line on my mother's side of pretty strong women. My mother was divorced when I was three and became a city planner in the days when there were few women in the field. She's a brilliant woman. So I always had this role model that you can do whatever you want to do. The message was, 'Hey you're very smart and very capable, and you can do whatever you feel like doing.'"

Humorist Loretta LaRoche's family was funny and filled with pranksters, especially her Italian relatives. In the early years before her mother's divorce, she says, "I was the family mascot. We lived in a brownstone in Brooklyn and I lived with all those adults who egged me on. Mother would put me to bed at night and she'd fall asleep and I'd come downstairs and tap dance for people." For Loretta, her ability to act out her feelings with humor became an important coping strategy and led to her current work.

Activist and writer Janet Hagberg truly resonated with her adventurous Aunt Lillian. Before Lillian died, Janet visited her one day in a snowstorm and exclaimed, "Lillian, it's snowing, look at the snow—it's just beautiful." There was about six inches of snow on the ground and Lillian, age eighty-one, said, "Let's go driving in it." Janet says that they slid around, practically doing donuts and having a grand time. Aunt Lil's *joie de vivre* modeled creative freedom for Janet.

Poet and author Awiakta, because of her blended Cherokee, Appalachian, and Celtic heritage, received some wonderful mentoring, especially from the women in her family. She says that the best career guidance she ever got was to stay close to her roots. Those words are responsible for the uniqueness and direction of her work today. Awiakta says, "As a child, I was always interested in international events, and the context of life. But in 1945, when I was nine years old, these interests became intensely personal—the atomic bomb was dropped on Hiroshima. Before then, only a few top scientists and government officials had known the 'secret' of what was being made at Oak Ridge. Now the world knew. The atom's power to destroy life was horrifying, and the nuclear reactor that split the atom was virtually in my family's backyard.

"What did it all mean for the world, for us? I listened to the elders talk about this question of how to use nuclear energy for peace. I thought about these questions too and began to peer into the nature of the atom myself. Thirty years later, I put my cumulative thoughts into my first book, *Abiding Appalachia: Where Mountain and Atom Meet.*"

Awiakta's mother also taught her about the importance of work as service: "My mother started me off very early in the tradition that what you do also needs to be good for the community. When I said I wanted to be a poet when I grew up, she said, 'That's good—and what will you do for the people?' So I got the idea very early on that how my work fit into the whole was very important.

A lot of young girls have looked to their career paths and have said they'd like to be chief. There's been a change in the limits people see.

—WILMA MANKILLER, FIRST WOMAN CHIEF OF THE CHEROKEE NATION

Both parents also taught me to have faith in God, a sense of humor, and that strength comes from heritage and coping with adversity."

This service value was also connected to policy making: "Entitlement to be strong and speak my mind came from the women around me in Appalachia, women who continued to manifest the ancient traditions of the Cherokee and the Celt. Originally, both cultures had been matrilineal and essentially egalitarian. Women had a central place in the home and the council. So did men—there was a balance. Despite the later imposition of patriarchal norms and the erasure of these matrilineal traditions from textbooks, the traditions are still alive and growing in the minds of many women and men." Awiakta's work merges the needs of Mother Earth and society with respect for the wisdom teachings of all peoples, with the necessity for both genders to manage progress and save the environment. That visionary nine-year-old girl who peered into the atom now tells stories to wake us up to our universal difficulties and call us to action.

Barbara Waugh's lifetime commitment to activism had its roots in her family as well. As Barbara says, "My mom and dad were always true to themselves, and they were my mentors in this respect. We were the only family on the block in our working-class neighborhood that went to the library. Our church got its first black Christian when my parents brought their African friend. In addition, my dad almost lost his job thirty years ago when, as a senior vice president, he insisted on alcohol recovery programs for employees with drinking problems, followed by a second chance, instead of an automatic firing. My mom also took a stand against domestic abuse when she called her neighbor's husband and told him if he ever laid a hand on his wife again, he would have to answer to her. Her friends told her that he would probably come and kill her for this. Her response was that this would not be a bad way to die—defending a friend." No wonder Barbara says that "being true to me is always inventing outside the box," or why possibilities intrigue her so.

For artist Carmella Yager, the lives of her grandmothers activated an important personal direction for her own career: "Both my grandmothers painted and inspired me. Yet their choices were different and they were not totally, 100 percent, committed to being artists. I think this influenced me to want to make a whole-hearted commitment to being a fine arts painter. Otherwise, how could I seriously and sincerely hope to make paintings of substance? I knew I could not casually make this trip. The journey seems at times arduous, but some of the views are pure glory."

Challenge: YOUR CREATIVE HERITAGE

Take a moment and think back to your family of origin. Were they creative? Were they supportive of your uniqueness and its expression? What kinds of encouraging and discouraging messages about your creativity did you get at home as a child? Did you get a sense of what you were naturally good at? Did your home life build or undermine your self-confidence? Who was the most supportive person of all in your family? What did you learn from him or her? What is the legacy of women in your family and how have these scripts shaped your choices? Did your mother thwart or express her creativity, and what impact has her behavior had on your creative courage? Write down any key concepts that you uncover and decide if you want these beliefs in your future. Remember, you are in charge now. Also, if your family experience was traumatic or painful, you may need to get some professional help in resolving your past, so you can move forward with more creative energy.

Seeking Out Role Models and Advisors

In the process of writing this book, I've had the opportunity to meet many of the women whose books or careers have served as guiding lights for me. I especially want to thank Sarah Ban Breathnach for telling me, "And just remember that the work knows more than you do—thank God." As I experienced this work reshaping itself almost daily and continually surprising me, her words kept me sane and trusting. I am most grateful.

As I mentioned earlier, I am a fan of Brenda Ueland, author of *If You Want to Write: A Book of Art, Independence, and Spirit.* Her first chapter is titled "Everybody is talented, original, and has something important to say." Brenda's words have kept me centered many a time. Author Janet Hagberg is also a fan: "Brenda's book was just a turnaround for me. She broke all the rules and she encourages you to do the same and write in your own way." Janet's book on writing, *Wrestling with Angels,* represents a second generation of Brenda's style of work. Janet actually met Brenda before her death, when she sent Brenda a letter and received an invitation to visit.

Janet recalls Brenda's words during that visit: "The most important thing she said to me was, 'Never be afraid, never,' in that dramatic voice of hers." Janet, who has taught writers to write from the soul, knows all too well the importance of faith and fearlessness as part of the creative process.

When I asked writer, photographer, and artist Maureen Murdock if she ever had a female mentor, she recalled a neighbor who influenced her in her early thirties: "My neighbor was Adelaide Fogg, who was a fairly well-known painter. She's dead now. But on Sunday mornings, my ex-husband would take care of the kids and I would go and sit on her front porch and we would paint. This went on for about three months and it was just an extraordinary experience for me, because she was really the first person who gave me permission to paint. And that was very healing."

Designer Sigrid Olsen attended Montserrat College of Art in Beverly, Massachusetts, where she studied photography, graphic design, painting, and printmaking, all of which she uses in her business today. After art school, she moved to Rockport, Massachusetts, a dramatic, rocky, quaint summer resort town, and set up a cottage design business. Fortuitously, she met her original business partner, Peter, there in Rockport. Peter had been in the garment industry and encouraged her to develop a business using prints. As Sigrid says, "He had a feeling for it after seeing the prints in Hawaii and he was right. I had always thought about prints for home furnishings, but he prompted me to focus on clothing. Then Peter met our financial partner in a restaurant. It was a miracle, and he showed him some of my early prints on clothing. That

> Being with real people who warm us, who endorse and exhault our creativity, is essential to the flow of the creative life. Otherwise we freeze.... When women are out in the cold, they tend to live on fantasies instead of action.
> —Clarissa Pinkola Estés, Jungian Analyst and Writer

partner got excited and he's still with us." Sigrid describes Peter as an idea person who always gave her too much to do, yet Sigrid was gutsy enough to follow his leads. For example, one day, Peter told her about a man in upstate New York who would print her fabric. So she went to see this man and "ended up mixing the ink myself in these huge buckets, instead of the egg cartons I was using before. He had these giant industrial blenders for mixing the silk screen inks. It was amazing to me—and I wasn't afraid—instead I was really excited." Sigrid continues to love learning new things but says now she hires "experts" to expand her repertoire.

Designer Joanne Rossman needed a job after impulsively leaving her abusive first husband one day. With a fat lip and a big shiner, she went to Joseph Magnin, a beautiful department store, and stood in front of Lillian Gilbert, the manager. Lillian said to her, "You look like hell." But after hearing Joanne's story, Lillian hired Joanne as a stock girl and told her not to go back to her husband. "So I worked as a stock girl for three weeks," remembers Joanne, "and Lillian took a liking to me. She became both my mentor and my tormentor. She was difficult, wonderful, and a real taskmaster, but she taught me everything and believed in me. She then sent me to buyers' school and I became a buyer, thanks to Lillian." This connection gave Joanne her first taste of business and sparked her confidence.

Ceramist Rosette Gault had hoped to find a mentor in graduate school but didn't. Still, as an undergraduate at the University of Colorado, she recalls a panel where women artists such as Judy Chicago and Miriam Shapiro spoke about the realities for women in the arts. Their guidance helped Rosette stay on course: "They talked about their struggle through graduate school and how to get through the pecking order and deal with the male mindset. I am really thankful for that panel experience. When I came up against those issues, I would think to myself, well, if Miriam can get through this and Judy could make it, so can I. I'm just going to have to hang tough and stick with it."

Later in her career in Seattle, Rosette sought out Jean Griffith, the head of Pottery Northwest, as a mentor because Rosette was attracted by Jean's serenity. At that time, Rosette was involved in setting up educational programs, and Jean helped her navigate through some stormy seas. "There were some things I did out of idealism that were misunderstood by other people," says Rosette. "Jean helped me to figure out a way to get out of the situation gracefully. She didn't berate me, and I learned from it." When Rosette got into a salary dispute with the art school she directed, even though she had saved the school from dying and built a strong team, Jean helped her from behind the scenes to step down with dignity. Two years later when Jean took a sabbatical, she hired Rosette as her replacement, which Rosette says felt like a real affirmation of her growth.

Jean also introduced Rosette to Lamar Harrington, a ceramics book author and arts community leader. Rosette says that as a new graduate student, she never really got to know Lamar because she was too frightened to talk with her. But one day, Rosette got up her nerve, approached Lamar, whom she noticed sitting in the local café, and asked her, "What advice do you have for young women?" Lamar told her that her one regret was that she hadn't gotten started sooner. Then Rosette remembers Lamar saying, "Just get up and do your thing and speak your truth. It's as simple as that." Gratefully, Rosette remembers Lamar helping her with her early writing projects, giving Rosette trust in her ability. By inviting these two elder women mentors into her life, Rosette gained important knowledge and expertise.

Passion powers our creative engines and keeps them running through the long haul. Guides can help us process the ebb and flow of our creative cycles along our personal, unique journey. In the early stages of writing *Leading From Your Soul*, Janet Hagberg was interviewing a college professor who had been a mentor to her: "Halfway through the interview on leadership, she said, 'Are you sure you want to write this book?'

"And I said, 'How can you tell?' My professor then said, 'I just don't feel passion from you about this book. What do you really want to write? Go write that one first.' She was right. So I ended up writing not a book on leadership but a long chapter and put it in the revision of *Real Power*. That felt great. It wasn't time to write the other book yet."

> Successful people realize the importance of a mentor or an advocate.
> —DONNA BROOKS AND LYNN BROOKS, WRITERS

> The degree to which you support and acknowledge yourself will be the degree to which you receive support.
> —SANAYA ROMAN, WRITER

For women whose creativity is not honored at home, the outer world of school and community offers the possibility of more encouraging guides. As we have noted before, teachers have incredible power to influence the self-esteem and creative development of their students. For Diane Ericson, the attention of her fifth grade teacher was a profound turning point for her: "In the fifth grade, I had a tall, beautiful teacher who had been a commercial artist. I remember being overwhelmed by this woman, as she was incredibly talented. One day, she pulled me aside and told me that my art was really special and that this was a gift I would have my whole life. Having someone you really admire outside your family take that kind of interest in you at that age is very significant."

For creative arts consultant Donna Luther, a nun at her Catholic school inspired her tremendously, and they are friends to this day. As Donna says, "I'm probably in music and drama today because of her." Encouragement from the outside often helps women resist the misguided fears of their parents. It fascinates me that both Diane and Donna teach creativity classes today and encourage self-expression in a potpourri of forms, including the arts.

Writer C. Diane Ealy has had some outstanding guides, beginning with her family: "My family is always supportive. They don't always understand what I'm doing, but they stay supportive. They always ask, 'Are you happy?'" In graduate school at the University of Pittsburgh, a male professor cultivated her many interests. Diane recalls, "It wasn't so much the subject area we discussed as much as when he looked at me, I knew I was an intelligent person. He validated me constantly and gave me things to read. He also kept trying to steer me into interpersonal communications when I was focused on mass communications. So he knew long before I did what was right for me."

In the mid-1970s, when Diane was studying to be a therapist, she heard Jean Houston speak at a conference at Berkeley: "When I heard Jean speak, I was absolutely blown away. This woman was saying things about what this society was going through that when I said them in high school were dismissed. So here's this woman standing in front of a group of 2,000 people talking about things that I had stopped talking about—but saying them in more positive ways. I thought, 'I've got to get to know her better.'" Diane then went to a workshop in Santa Cruz with Jean and invited her to become her dissertation mentor and Jean said "Yes." It was a profound relationship for Diane, for, she says, "I trusted her in a way that I don't usually trust people. So when she would do these phenomenal deep trance guided imagery exercises, I would allow myself to go to pretty amazing levels."

After working on her book *The Woman's Book of Creativity* for more than twelve years, Diane felt discouraged about getting it published. But an angel was in her future. Nancy Solomon, who works at the Center for Creative Photography in Arizona and with whom Diane did a video on women photographers, became Diane's advocate, connecting her with the owners of Beyond Words Publishing, who published her book.

In addition to the support of her famous family, Lucia Capacchione had several key mentors in her youth outside her family. One was a well-known painter who became an advocate. Lucia commented: "He allowed me, even though I was quite young, into an adult painting class at Otis Art Institute on Saturdays, and that saved my life through high school. He really showed me what a mentor relationship could be. His style of mentoring was to bring out the best in his students. He didn't want to create clones and he didn't want us copying his style. He wanted us to follow our own style and that was very, very wonderful."

Help comes in all kinds of forms. Sarah Ban Breathnach dedicated *Simple Abundance* to her agent, Chris Tomasino, and her daughter, Katie. Sarah discovered Chris through a connection from a publicist. *"Simple Abundance* was rejected thirty times in two years," says Sarah, "and Chris stayed with me the whole time—she always believed in me." Sarah says she just acted as if she had a contract and kept writing, despite people telling her to abandon the project. And Chris kept her on track, as Sarah recounts: "Every time the next round of rejections came through, Chris would say, 'Go cry tonight and then get up tomorrow and get back to work.'"

Sarah also benefited greatly from Chris's wisdom about editors, and she recalls Chris's expert advice: "The worst thing that can happen to any writer is to get an editor who doesn't *get* the book.

> No person is your friend who demands your silence, or denies your right to grow.
> —ALICE WALKER, AUTHOR

It has to have the right editor. The right editor is out there and we will find her. I swear to God we will find her." After twenty-eight rejections, Chris came to her and said that Liv Blumer at Warner books loved *Simple Abundance* and wanted her to do it as a meditation book for women like *Meditations for Women Who Do Too Much*. Sarah laughed and dismissed the idea. But then Sarah sought out another kind of guidance—prayer and mediation—and said to the Great Creator: "Why are you not leading me to the right editor out there?" The response that echoed in her heart was, "I already have. Can we please get to work now?" So for the next two years, Sarah rewrote the book into daily meditations, Liv published it, and the bestseller list awaited.

Jan Brett also got some excellent advice from an expert. As a young illustrator, she recalls visiting with editors in New York and showing them her portfolio, wishing for some truthful input: "All of the editors were very nice. I think they're afraid that you're going to jump out a window, so they never say anything bad. I had lots of drawings of animals and one time this editor said to me, 'Children's books are really about children. You should have children in your portfolio. Take all your animals and just pretend they have a big zipper on them and unzip their fur suits so that there's a kid inside.' That was great advice but challenging, for children are hard to draw as their expressions are so natural. And then I had another editor tell me not to do long stories—just short ones. He also encouraged me to write my own stories and to remember that they have to have real emotion in them because children are very discriminating and that if it doesn't have the whole gamut of emotions in it they won't be interested."

This kind of honest, helpful advice from the experts dramatically increases your chances for success. You have to be willing to be true to your own creative instincts, yet open to the knowing of people you can trust. When I wrote my audiotape, I had several people listen to a rough copy. A training colleague of mine, Mimi McGrath, suggested that I have other people's voices on the tape responding to the exercises. It was a great idea, worked really well, and supported my purpose. A critical skill for many creative women is discernment—knowing whose advice is from the heart

Take control of your destiny. Believe in yourself. Ignore those who try to discourage you. Avoid negative sources, people, places, things and habits. Don't give up and don't give in.
—WANDA CARTER, WRITER

and really meant to be helpful, and avoiding folks who pull you away from your intentions and may be trying to undermine your achievement.

Challenge: GUIDANCE LIFE REVIEW

Take a few minutes to think of all of the influential people outside your family who have served as advisors to you. What did you learn from them? What messages did they convey and how has their influence impacted your decisions? Were you the victim of bad advice or mentoring? What kind of guidance was most helpful and illuminating? How do you learn best?

After reviewing your relationships with life guides, you are now ready to brainstorm about what kinds of positive guides and support systems you want to incorporate into your future. What kind of guidance do you need now? Do you want a small circle of intimate relationships or a large expansive network of people to interact with? What kinds of people are you repelled by or resistant to? What kinds of individuals, groups, or organizations feel comfortable to you?

As C. Diane Ealy says in *The Woman's Book of Creativity,* "At the most basic level, supporting others without nurturing ourselves depletes energy necessary for developing creativity." If our inner circles or chance encounters don't reap the kinds of guides we need, hiring a coach is an option. A great coach keeps you accountable and inspires growth and positive change. Writer Carol Frenier networked her way to experienced coach Sydney Rice, who offered to coach Carol through the process of writing her book. Carol's advice is that if anyone of quality believes in your project and offers to help, accept them as a gift. What Sydney did that was most beneficial was teach her that if she made a comment about something, she needed to be very specific. Carol says, "From the first draft to the last, only about 5 percent of the quotes survived. Sydney encouraged me to focus on my voice and cut the academic, preachy stuff out."

To be coached, we have to be willing to be open to honest feedback. Dr. Lesley Shore also appreciated useful input on her writing: "Some people seem totally unable to give feedback. I mean, I love pats on the head, and I used to always do everything to get approval. Writing is really important to me because it's the first time in my life when I really actually wanted criticism. I wanted somebody to tell me what was wrong with it so I could revise it." It takes courage to be open to critique and scrutiny, but it also motivates us to master our craft and reach greater standards of quality.

Challenge: IDENTIFYING YOUR STYLISTIC NEEDS

If you were to hire a guide, what would you tell them about how to communicate with you in a way that is most supportive? What approaches work best for you? What styles of guidance repel you or cause you to rebel? Notice your personal patterns as you answer these questions. Summarize your answers into a guidance profile for yourself highlighting what you need and how you can best work with your issues.

Initiating or Joining a Group

Groups can offer support for your creative process. I found it very interesting that most of the women I profiled were not active in professional associations or formal networks. In fact, several people commented that they had even been ignored by their professional associations, despite their unique accomplishments. I always advise clients to shop around for a comfortable network for themselves, to create their own collegial connections, or to form a Success Team. As some of the women in this book are introverts, they tend to find networking a challenge. A room full of extroverts all talking at once can be most intimidating to quieter folks. Yet too much isolation can undermine your professional goals and limit the growth of your business. The Internet has created some fascinating ways for introverts to get connected through forums and e-mail with easy approaches to strangers. Marcia Yudkin's book *Marketing Online* is a good reference on how to get started.

Networking expert Lynne Waymon, once a shy child, is now an evolved extrovert. She teaches an incredible workshop on networking and has written several books on the subject with her sister, Anne Baber. Lynne has some interesting comments about men and women as networkers, though she is cautious about stereotyping. "Many men are more comfortable exchanging facts and data. They do a competitive networking saying, 'I have this and I have that,' establishing their niche or their place. Women often do a bit more sympathetic listening, drawing out the other person. Generally women are less comfortable making a strategic plan to become visible. It seems to go against everything that we've been taught to do, but we need to do it. I have women make a list of ten people who could help them promote their business, and women are initially squeamish about this. I also advise people to talk about their successes in a comfortable way that teaches other people what to count on them for—their competence and character. I also want to teach them to connect people with other people; it's a high level kind of networking."

Networking is a mutual process of communication and sharing. It is a necessary part of connecting your creative work to the marketplace. If you want to get your work out into the world, honestly assess your networking skill level and improve your comfort zone. I highly recommend Lynne's materials to assist you. But, be true to your own style. I was active in a large number of networks before I became ill, whereupon I dropped almost all of them. In reconnecting slowly, I thought carefully about which groups were nurturing as well as productive, and selected a few that felt like good choices. I usually avoid giant network meetings where I just feel lost and rarely accomplish much of anything.

What often works better than structured professional organizations are groups you organize yourself. My Sophia Circle of eight women engaged in creative pursuits as well as personal and spiritual growth is currently my main support group. We meet once a month around the full moon and encourage each other's original unfolding. For five years, Maureen Murdock was in a monthly

> Call it a clan, call it a network, call it a tribe, call it a family: Whatever you call it, whoever you are, you need one.
> —JANE HOWARD, BUSINESSWOMAN

photography critique group that reviewed each member's work and progressed to doing shows together. While this group has disbanded, Maureen still meets with one of the women every few weeks to share creative work and mutual encouragement.

After she moved to Boston, designer Joanne Rossman started a group for women working in isolation. Her group included a writer, a jeweler, another designer, a quilter, a sweater maker, and a sculptor. "The prerequisite for getting together," says Joanne, "was that you had to work on your own, and be female, because men already have lots of support." Three of the women had invitational showings together and became quite successful. While the group served its time, the women all remain friends.

Joanne is very generous with what she knows and was startled by the withholding behavior among artists that she encountered in the Northeast. Yet, she is clear about her values and how she chooses to operate: "I was stunned to find that if you call someone in the garment industry on the east coast and say to them, 'I saw the most wonderful piece of yours where you used this incredible taffeta as a facing, could you tell me where you got it?' most of them will never tell you. I've always shared where I find the things I buy because I figure it's going to come back to me in a million ways." This spirit of cooperation has made Joanne, as she says, "rich with friends."

Several years ago, I developed Creativity Circles for aspiring creative women using the principles in this book in which we create a safe haven laced with brainstorming, accountability, and specific goals to attain. These circles came into being to encourage women to live their dreams by giving them both the tools and the camaraderie of supportive sisters.

Setting up a network of guides is an important positive life choice. We can't change the past, but I hope that the numerous examples of guidance in all forms shared here will spark your own thoughts about what you really desire. I should also mention that a large percentage of the women I interviewed had done considerable personal growth work with psychotherapists, massage therapists, spiritual directors, coaches, acupuncturists, and other healers. As self-awareness and your ability to value your insights represent key components of creative evolution, all of these adventures in self-discovery and healing will facilitate the clarity of your creative channel. You must make self-care a top priority in your life, and selecting the right guides as role models helps you advance in the direction of your creative goals.

Challenge: DESIGNING YOUR GUIDANCE OPTIONS

In coaching, I often tell my clients to "design me," which means having them tell me specifically what they do and don't need from our relationship. Here are a list of assorted concepts to help you to get crystal clear about what kinds of guidance you want to create for yourself. Check off any of these learning options that interest you.

1. New skills
2. Special information
3. Classes
4. Groups—what kind?
5. A buddy or partner
6. A mentor or role model
7. Psychotherapy or another kind of therapeutic intervention
8. A coach
9. Contacts or connections
10. Resources such as books, tapes, videos, online information
11. Relationships with peers in your areas of interest
12. Spiritual practice, support group, or organization
13. Some system of structure or a schedule
14. New sources of inspiration
15. Formal education or a degree

For each option you checked off, expand it and define exactly what you want. For example, in taking a class, are you most interested in meeting other students, building a relationship with the teacher, experimenting with a new medium, having your work critiqued, or learning marketing information? If you are looking for a relationship with a particular kind of guide, make a list of your criteria. Can one person satisfy your needs or are you looking for several people? Summarize your insights into a list of your needs and desires. Then visualize the kind of guide who could help you to get the support you need for the next step on your journey. You deserve to have her (or him) in your life.

To start the process of finding a guide or a group, begin looking around you. Talk to trusted friends and colleagues and gather a list of possible people or resources. Visit classes or schools or go check out the work of a possible mentor. But, above all, follow your intuition. Your creative energy is precious, and you must pursue the right kind of respectful support.

Guiding Others

Many of the women in this book guide others. One of those is singer Rebecca Parris, a self-appointed guide to people of all ages. In fact, one of her singing students gave her a key chain that says "Mother Magnet." Rebecca explains, "I am a mother figure to a lot of people—I'm definitely a missionary." Rebecca's house is filled with students as she cooks, coaches, and catalyzes them to greater growth. She buys spiritual books and hands them out and even sent me home with a copy of *Conversations with God—Book Two*. She recently adopted a woman as her daughter and feels a responsibility to support and heal others. She teaches at two jazz camps where she inspires creative expression, builds self-esteem, and urges students to follow their dreams. One of the courses she teaches is called "Finding Yourself through Your Lyrics" and Rebecca loves it when a student discovers more about who he or she is through a piece of music.

Empowering others fuels Rebecca's creative fire. She says, "My music is about delivering and receiving. I want to see the people. I want to create a power relationship with the audience. A real power relationship is a constant feed and that's one of the biggest talents I have which I try to make the most of." Winner of numerous Boston Music Awards, Rebecca has an astonishingly beautiful voice. Shirley Horn says, "Rebecca's voice sets her apart from any other vocalist on record today. A mood that transcends the ordinary, that in one moment exudes warmth and is poignant, in another driving hard and swinging."

When you experience Rebecca either one on one or as an audience member, you know she's connected with you with all her heart, her soul, and her cherished jazz. Rebecca's CD *Spring* was my constant writing companion all during this book.

Like Rebecca, consider your power in the world to serve as a guide. When your niece shows you a picture, a friend wants you to listen to a poem she's written, or a colleague has a new idea to share, before you respond, wake up and pay attention! Don't just react automatically or unconsciously. They are sharing their creativity with you, and your response to their creation has the potential to help or hinder their confidence. Think about how you would like to be treated or heard if the tables were turned. Honor their efforts above all. Then ask them to talk about the significance of their work and what kind of feedback would be most helpful.

We are all guides to someone in our lives and therefore we have opportunities to nurture and support others. It is not appropriate to condemn and devalue other people's innovations. We can express our honest opinion, but with reverence for the person's courage to express herself. A world where each of us sees our chance to play guide as a sacred role will help to heal the scars of creative destruction that too many of us have already experienced. It is my hope that these examples urge you to encourage and protect creative expression in people of all ages.

> When indeed shall we learn that we are all related one to the other, that we are all members of one body?
> —HELEN KELLER, ACTIVIST

Selecting Empowering Partnerships
and Alliances

Whether or not to work with others in your creative
endeavors is an important decision, requiring both self-
assessment and the careful selection of collaborators.

Keys

- Deciding Whether and How to Affiliate
  with Others
- Assessing Your Collaborative Potential
- Avoiding Disasters
- Choosing the Right People
- Building Your Team
- Freeing Up Your Creative Energy
- Partnering with Significant Others
- Collaborating in the Future

Surround yourself with people you can learn from.
Don't try to do it all on your own. I don't believe
I could have possibly accomplished what I've
done without the help of everyone else."

—SIGRID OLSEN, FASHION DESIGNER

In this time of mergers and acquisitions, Internet commerce, and technological freedoms, innovative collaborations comprise a global theme. So the choice to work alone or join forces with one or more people in a creative endeavor becomes an important question, especially in the "bigger is better" mentality of mega-resources. In order to decide which model suits you, you need to know yourself and how you operate. For some people, working alone is a joy; for others, the isolation drains their energy and motivation.

Deciding Whether and How to Affiliate with Others

Collaborating with others adds a different dimension to the creative process. One of the advantages is the old idea that "two heads are better than one." Working closely with others on a creative project expands the available net of ideas, skills, and experience. Pat Miller and Barbara Baekgaard have run three successful businesses together as faithful partners. Sigrid Olsen has gathered a team of creatives and business folks to work with her designing fashions. Alison Shaw and her three partners purchased a commercial building together in Martha's Vineyard for their studio and retail spaces. Lydia Shire and Deborah Henson-Conant each have business partners they trust and count on. Brenda Laurel's start-up company Purple Moon began as a spin-off but is now securing investors for its next phase. Sidra Stone partners with husband Hal Stone in marriage, psychotherapy, writing, and training, and Jan Brett and Chris Madden have husbands who help manage their businesses. Marilyn and Bill Veltrop came together because they each wanted a business partner as well as a life partner, and wouldn't settle for less. Rebecca Parris' friends and family believed so strongly in her first album that they donated funds and expertise to the project.

A partnership consists of two or more persons engaged in the same business and sharing its profits and risks. What I call "strategic alliances" function as a union, a joining, or a close association with a common objective. These can be much more casual than a partnership, such as someone who admires your work, sends you business, and you return the favor. It could also be a gallery that exhibits your work, or an alliance between two complementary businesses. Alliances between companies or individuals can be project-based or experimental.

If you are thinking about a creative alliance or partnership, your first inquiry is at what stage, if any, of the creative process do you want participation? Do you want to co-create a sweater, a painting, or a song with one other person or a group? Or do you want to protect your creative freedom to develop the vision and execute it without interference?

After you've created your vision, do you then want help with marketing, manufacturing, or securing investors?

Each kind of relationship has different parameters. I've seen many women in the fledgling stage of their careers grab another woman as a business partner simply so they didn't have to be out there alone. Many of these relationships, built on lack or weakness as opposed to compatible skills, fizzled in an angry smoke of uncommunicated expectations and disappointments. The urge to merge has both healthy and unhealthy aspects to it, and mistakes can interfere with your creative flow. Remember this saying: "Hungry people make poor shoppers." Never agree to an alliance out of desperation; wait or explore other options for yourself. Take the time to consider carefully what's best for you. Many of the women who have experienced collaborative disasters didn't follow their intuition about the situation and redirect things in time.

> Until a woman has given herself permission to be fabulous, she will not find herself with partners who promote her ability to be so.
> —MARIANNE WILLIAMSON, WRITER

Assessing Your Collaborative Potential

Before you embark on a partnership or alliance for yourself or even if you're in one already, take the time to complete the following

Challenge. While this is a lengthy exercise, it will increase your awareness of your natural abilities and vulnerabilities in collaborative relationships. Successful partnerships and alliances depend on complete honesty, open communication, self-awareness, and a commitment to resolve conflicts for mutual benefit.

Challenge: YOUR COLLABORATION PROFILE

The following questions are meant to raise your consciousness of the important issues to ponder before you initiate a collaboration, or to help you improve your relationship with potential or present partners. Be totally candid in your answers.

1. Have you ever been called any of the following adjectives or do you know them to be true about yourself? Check off any adjectives that apply. Note that many of these adjectives are purposely negative to help you confront your weaknesses.

Bitch	Too quiet
Wimp	Cold
Pushover	Insensitive
Arrogant	Unforgiving
Passive-aggressive	Fickle
Evil	Conflict-avoider
Vicious	Mysterious
Indecisive	Flip-flop decision maker
Vindictive	Untrustworthy
Caustic	Loner
Passive	Team player
Bossy	Hermit-like
Domineering	Collaborative
Unfeeling	Forthright
Overly nice	Sensitive
Laid back	Clear communicator

Trustworthy	Likable
Person of integrity	Engaging
People person	Focused, hard-working

Group your adjectives together and analyze the patterns. Now, tell the truth. If someone else thinks you're a loner, is it true or false? Sometimes we are accused by other people of things that simply are not true. Which adjectives are accurate and which are not? Sort them out by category. For example, if you have a pattern of adjectives that point to being bossy, domineering, and insensitive, then collaborations could prove difficult for you without some planning and coaching. Note your strengths and the positive qualities that you bring to the table in relationships. Partnering is a match-up process.

2. Are you by nature an extrovert or an introvert? Extroverts love to process ideas with others and feel energized by groups, while introverts think of plenty of ideas on their own and can work for long hours independently. Some of us are also a balance of the two extremes. Perhaps we are extroverted at work but more introverted at home or in a transition of some sort, needing different kinds of experiences with people. Log your behavior for two weeks and see what kinds of interactions you do or don't want with others.

3. Honestly review your relationship history with partners, groups, or organizations. If you have a history of failed partnerships, what makes you think you even want to partner with someone? How do you need to change to make a relationship work? On the other hand, if you have a long history of enduring collaborations, that's an encouraging sign. What kinds of people have you worked best with? How well have you managed conflicts with others? Also, how do you connect and disconnect from relationships? Do you end things on a

friendly note or in a courtroom? Your relationship record has much to teach you.

4. Are you a good listener or a poor one? What is your communication style—quiet, succinct, aggressive, or terse? Do people usually understand you or is being misunderstand a common experience for you? Do you need to learn some improved ways of communicating effectively?

5. Are you able to assertively express your thoughts and feelings to others or do you hide your real opinions?

6. Are you an effective negotiator? Can you mediate on your own behalf as well as for others?

7. What irritates you most about other people? How well do you handle these challenges?

8. What characteristics in yourself do you feel most defensive or vulnerable about? Think back to a few times when people have really "pushed your buttons" and how you handled it.

9. Do you enjoy the people aspects of managing others—advising, training, listening, joint problem solving? If not, spare yourself and them the agony of working for you. But if you want to be a positive people manager, get some coaching or training.

10. What kinds of people energize you and what kinds of people drain you?

11. What kinds of social events or leisure activities do you enjoy sharing with people?

12. What parts of your work do you love and want to do on your own?

13. What kinds of work do you enjoy sharing with others and in what format?

14. Are you able to delegate tasks effectively?

15. What tasks in your work or business do you least enjoy or truly dislike and would prefer to have someone else handle? What kinds of skills or experience in another

person would complement your talents and preferences? Do you really want a business partner or just a referral source or another kind of affiliation?

16. What models of partnership appeal to you? Describe your vision of what kind of model would work well for you, given your personality, work style, needs, and relationship history.

17. How well do you handle money? What sales and marketing abilities do you have? What kind of knowledge do you have about accounting, bookkeeping, or financial planning? Are you a tightwad or overly generous? How do you or have you handled financial negotiations in other relationships? What kinds of safeguards do you need around money to make sure that you don't get taken advantage of? Do you have a reputation for cheating people? What kind of financial skills do you want to learn or need help with? What are your "hot buttons" around money? Do you have a prosperity mindset or a scarcity mindset?

From these questions, compile a list of both strengths and potential pitfalls for yourself. Use them as a guide to making decisions about potential collaborations. Whatever your pitfalls, either fix them—for example, learn to become an good listener—or enlist the support of others. Review the above questions on a regular basis and, if possible, share your answers with potential or existing partners or collaborators. They will prevent many of the stumbling blocks that ruin relationships and businesses.

Avoiding Disasters

There are many tragic stories of both personal and business relationships that ended as lawsuits or feuds, costly both emotionally and financially. Several of the women I interviewed had tales of betrayal and dishonesty in their history but chose not to include them in this book. Yet there are clearly some lessons to learn from them. First, integrity and respect are essential ingredients of any positive partnership. If one person lies, withholds information, or blackmails the other person, disaster is the result. In my opinion, the vital foundation for a solid relationship is self-knowledge on the part of each person involved and a commitment to joint abundance. Some people should never be partners with anyone; they can't be trusted to work collaboratively, to tell the truth, or to negotiate conflicts with respect and mutuality. One woman told the story of a male partner who had so many secrets from his partners that he was constantly getting caught in his own lies.

In my professional practice, I have coached numerous potential business partners out of teaming up together. I often use the Myers-Briggs Type Indicator, an inventory of preferences, as a discussion tool, and have both partners compare scores and work styles. I also use the Collaboration Profile to help me to screen out potential conflict areas with them. (While this profile is comprehensive, be sure to get any legal or business advice you need before moving forward.) Sometimes it also helps to "try on" a relationship first, that is, work on one project together and see how you cooperate and communicate.

> If you do not tell the truth about yourself you cannot tell it about other people.
> —VIRGINIA WOOLF, WRITER

Choosing the Right People

Successful partnerships and alliances thrive with common values and principles. Three-time business partners and friends, Pat Miller and Barbara Baekgaard, now co-owners of Vera Bradley Designs, illustrate the essentials of working together in harmony and exhilaration. As a flower fanatic myself, I was delighted to receive my first flowered Vera Bradley pocketbook from my brother and sister-in-law who live in Fort Wayne, Indiana, home of the now multimillion-dollar Vera Bradley Designs. My pocketbook was light and colorful and more than big enough to carry all of my stuff around. I became a devotee; Vera Bradley bags became a favorite gift choice for myself and family members.

Their relationship began when Pat welcomed Barbara to her neighborhood twenty-four years ago. For their first venture, called Up Your Wall, Pat and Barbara hung wallpaper for eight years. They then shifted gears and sold other companies' clothing lines from home, sponsoring a trunk show twice a year.

In 1982, while awaiting a flight in the Atlanta airport, the two women noticed a lack of attractive feminine luggage among their fellow passengers. That observation sent them to the fabric store with $500 to purchase material to make soft-sided bags in feminine patterns. Initial products included a handbag, a duffel bag, and a garment bag. Now Vera Bradley Designs manufactures, designs, and distributes a full line of luggage, handbags, and accessories internationally. Future plans include doubling sales within the next four years.

I asked Pat and Barbara about the secrets of their successful and enduring partnership. They both replied in harmony: "We have a lot of respect for each other." Pat added that they "never keep score" and Barbara commented, "We've never embarrassed each other." They have one voice in public and incredible loyalty to one another. It is clear that they also enjoy each other's company and sharing the events of growing a business together. Pat said, "The other great thing about having a good partner is having an honest sounding board. Sharing ideas is invaluable."

When I asked them what strengths each of them brought to the relationship, Pat was quick to say, "Barbara's very, very creative and very people-oriented. She's also extremely outgoing, upbeat, moves fast, and makes decisions quickly. She gets things done." Barbara confirmed that neither one of them could have run the company alone. They each have had ups and downs in their lives and have picked up the slack for one another. Barbara also acknowledged Pat's expertise: "Pat was the one who suggested that we get a consultation with SCORE (Senior Corps of Retired Executives)—I would have just muddled along. Pat is great for finding the right answers and resources, especially on the business/financial end. But most important, we think alike."

Division of labor is another smart strategy for success. Pat and Barbara are involved in the community and are active on a number of boards. "It is important that we build strong community relationships," says Barbara. They also attend gift shows and network within their industry. "Our partnership allows us to split up the tasks," said Pat. Both women share a deep commitment to fight breast cancer. After the loss of a dear friend to this illness, Barbara

> The ultimate test of a relationship is to disagree but to hold hands.
> —Alexandra Penney, Writer

> The nice thing about teamwork is that you always have others on your side.
> —Margaret Carty, Writer

and Pat established the Vera Bradley Classic, an amateur golf and tennis competition that benefits breast cancer research and programs. This event is now a premier women's sporting event in Indiana.

Building Your Team

Pat and Barbara's solidarity extends to the work environment they've created with their employees, who feel like family. As owners, they encourage new ideas, celebrate pregnancies, and even tried to start an in-house day care center (but the governmental regulations proved insurmountable in their present building). As Barbara said, "We have so many people here that we trust to make decisions, and if they happen to make a wrong choice, we encourage them to just fix it." The sixty-two employees also serve as a test market for new designs. Pat stated emphatically, "We have a goal that Vera Bradley be one of the best businesses to work for in the country." This positive management model of incorporating high standards, empowering employees, and celebrating family and community forges a new standard in the business world.

The corporate offices in Wakefield, Massachusetts, of Sigrid Olsen, which designs women's clothing, reflects owner Sigrid Olsen's gift for leading a team. The offices impressed me with their welcoming ambiance laced with excitement about this booming $50 million enterprise. While I was waiting for Sigrid, a birthday party unfolded in the lobby for one of the employees. Their new offices are spacious and inviting, and people connect with each other in warmth and camaraderie.

Sigrid, a striking blonde, floated from task to task with poise and confidence. Like Pat and Barbara, Sigrid sets the tone for her company. I commented to her how friendly, egalitarian, and comfortable her company felt, and Sigrid conceded that they now need systems and departments, but that she's committed to preserving the feeling of community.

Sigrid sees one of her main jobs as holding the big picture for her group: "To be creative director of a company this size, I have to understand how it all fits together. And I didn't get there

> Alone we can do so little; together we can do so much.
> —HELEN KELLER, ACTIVIST

overnight. It happened over of period of fourteen years. In the beginning I did everything. I learned how to do the specs myself for the garments. I went over to the Orient and worked in the factories and packed boxes. I mastered using a computer, taking orders over the phone, and reading a financial statement—the whole thing. Everything I did in art school at Montserrat—the photography, the graphic design, the painting, and the printmaking—blended into a broad base of knowledge that I use now. So that when I'm working on my catalogs with photographers and graphic designers, we speak the same language. The fashion design I've learned on the job. I recommend to people to find out what comes naturally to you and if you do that well, you can find other people to do the pieces to support you. But you have to be willing to let go and delegate to other people. With my company, I've set up a system where if I have an idea, there's a process to go through to make it happen." Sigrid's commitment to treat everyone at all levels of the organization with respect and consideration, combined with her adventurous spirit, has manifested itself into a positive workplace.

Another talented collaborator is Pam Moore, who has happily flourished at Synectics for twenty-six years and is now a partner in her beloved enterprise. What inspires her daily is "an incredibly profound belief that I'm not only creative, but that I can help people discover their own creativity."

As a consultant and an extrovert, she helps clients generate new ideas and solutions, which in turn fuels Pam's creative energy as well. "I need other people to balance me as well as catalyze different styles of thinking," she acknowledges. "I love people and thrive on meeting all kinds of men and women from varied industries. Getting people talking, thinking, and connecting teaches me—I learn something." Synectics' consultants work in pairs to facilitate an interactive process with client companies, and Pam is a master of group creativity. One of Pam's passions is "product naming," and she has reconfigured her responsibilities to focus more of her energy on perfecting this art form. I asked Pam if she planned to write about her discoveries and, no surprise, she is working on an article with her friend Peggy as an initial collaborator. So far she

> As we give fully, unafraid to let others know the truth about ourselves, we receive unexpected rewards from unexpected sources.
> —HELENE LERNER-ROBBINS, WRITER

has concluded that women are often better namers than men because they are less literal and more comfortable living with ambiguity during the process. As a creativity conduit, Pam loves playing with people and their ideas, and she partners with others in almost every work activity. For balance, Pam loves quiet time at home with her husband and a few close friends, and enjoys cooking, dancing, and designing her own garden.

Photographer Alison Shaw felt claustrophobic running her entire photography business at her home on Martha's Vineyard and sought to find a community of other artists to share offices and exhibit space with her. After looking for six months, she received a phone call about a building for sale, a building she recognized and loved: "I went and saw the building the next morning and thought this is where I want to be. How am I going to do this? The owners said that there was a woman from Edgartown coming to look at it that afternoon. I didn't have a group together yet and felt discouraged. Later that day I had an appointment to see Catherine, a former student of mine, who wanted to show me some photographs. She came over, we shared photographs, and spent a long time drinking tea and talking—I really connected with her. Right before she left, she commented that it looked like I was outgrowing my space and I told her that I had seen a building I loved that morning, but that it was just beyond my reach. She said, 'That's funny, I looked at a place this afternoon.' *She* was the lady from Edgartown. This was like a message from God, we decided; but we had to get a group together. Catherine had a close friend, Adrianne, who does handpainted furniture, and I had a colleague, Betsy, whose work I respect. But, Betsy was away camping for four days and I couldn't reach her.

"The next morning, Catherine, Adrianne, and I got together for tea and scones. It was so different from how men might do it. We were really trying to feel each other out as human beings. But time was short, as there was another party that wanted to open an auto parts store in that space. The three of us bonded, and when Betsy came back, she clicked with us as well. What was so important for us was a sense of creative space—not just four cubicles." The four of them bought the building and relish the mutual sharing and collaboration.

Singer Rebecca Parris calls herself a "lousy loner," so she works with a team. With her manager and her best friend, Rebecca formed a record company to re-release her first three LPs onto CDs, as well as to set up a new Web site. This best friend, who moved to be close to Rebecca, is a cherished asset. "My best friend is an incredibly different human than I am. She's extremely organized and brighter than all-get-out in business. We rub off on each other in ways that are really awesome."

The isolation of writing often fuels a desire for collaboration. Barrie Dolnick writes regularly with two other women.

In New York, they meet once a week but they also do marathon writing trips. As Barrie says, "We just came back from two weeks of writing up in the Catskills. Usually we go on one trip a year and have been to Scotland, Cornwall, and Ireland, and we're planning a trip to Egypt. We go away for two and three weeks where we work together. We meditate and do rituals every day."

Networking expert Lynne Waymon writes with her sister who is halfway across the country. Her sister has a background in journalism and corporate communications and encouraged Lynne to try writing. Lynne was resistant at first: "It didn't sound like a barrel of fun to me because I like to be out with people and not sitting at the computer, but my sister convinced me that it would be wonderful experience." I asked her how they managed the process and she outlined their format: "We met face to face to develop a general direction and themes of chapters. Then we both independently did a lot of focus groups, interviewing people looking for stories and real-life verification of what actually goes on. Then we divided the chapters up and she'd say 'Okay, I'll do chapter 6 by March 1.' And I'd say 'Okay, I'll do chapter 4—that's the one I really like.' And then we'd trade these chapters back and forth until we had no idea who wrote what—they became our chapters." I asked her if they ever wrote intensively together and Lynne said, "A couple of times I've gone to her house when we've had a deadline because her children are all grown up and out. It's a little quieter scene than my house. One time, I was there for about ten days and we wrote from morning to night. I thought I was going to lose my mind." Lynne appreciates her sister's editorial expertise and now plans to

> Your playing small serves no one.
>
> —MARIANNE WILLIAMSON, WRITER

keep writing. Her sister actually helped her to achieve a triumph that Lynne may not have done by herself.

Freeing Up Your Creative Energy

An added benefit of partnerships and alliances is that they free up time so you can create. In addition to serving as illustrator Jan Brett's bouncer-of-sorts, husband Joe is also a musician with the Boston Symphony Orchestra. Jan travels with him to his concerts, and he accompanies her on book-signing tours, helping her manage the production, public relations, and organization. His managerial role frees her up to focus on illustrations, for as she says, "I'd rather draw than plan," and with Joe at her side as a true partner, she can.

For designer Diane Ericson, hiring assistants facilitates the growth of her business in the direction she desires. She told me, "I've just hired an experienced office manager to help me with my office. This is brand new for me. The message I got as a child was that something's wrong if you can't take care of all of this yourself. But I knew (a) that's not what I was interested in, or (b) what I'm good at. I've also hired an accountant/business consultant who is one of the most creative women I've ever met. I need these people to play with me." Diane shares her home with another woman and her daughter, who handle her household when Diane is on the road.

For aging specialist Miriam Nelson, collaborating with a writing partner, Sarah Wernick, allowed Miriam to stay focused on her area of expertise. When I asked Miriam how they got together, she told an interesting story: "I had been wanting to put a book together, but I was very busy with my research and I didn't know the publishing world at all. When Sarah wrote to me after reading about my findings on women in a journal article, her letter sat in my pile for about six weeks. Her husband is a colleague of mine. Finally I called her back, as I loved her writing style in the materials she had sent me. So we met and she knew all the stages of getting an agent, writing a proposal, and so on, and she was very excited about my work. So we began our collaboration."

Miriam makes an important point about alliances always being a risk—you never know how the relationship is really going to work out. Fortunately, Miriam and Sarah's dynamics harmonized. As Miriam says, "Sarah and I complemented each other very well as we're both really hard workers. We never held each other up. I was always working on material for the next section. Sarah was working on the previous chapter, and as soon as she was ready, I was ready, and we'd switch. We were always sort of leap-frogging. And we kept our sense of humor; it seems like we laughed the entire time we were writing. We always questioned each other. Sarah pushed and pushed—now wait, you said it that way, but you know, last week you said it a little differently, but it could be conceived from the outside looking in, that it's going in a different direction. We had that kind of dialogue." Like Pat and Barbara at Vera Bradley, Miriam and Sarah appreciate each other's contribution to the whole, and each tackles her own piece of a project.

Deborah Henson-Conant runs her music business with her partner Stephanie Zand and three other part-time people. Deborah says her most important professional support is Stephanie, especially for camaraderie. She loves the idea of a team and says many musicians who don't have one get a little crazy. "For Stephanie," Deborah says, "our relationship is particularly interesting because her success or failure depends on me. I'm her product. We're both on this adventure together, and it's important not to be alone." Deborah says she often has a hard time hanging onto her own accomplishments, and having Stephanie around helps to keep things in perspective. Stephanie also stays bonded to Deborah by phone during the four to five months a year that Deborah travels. Stephanie enables Deborah to play with new sounds while Stephanie handles the details.

Partnering with Significant Others

Sidra Stone and her husband Hal Stone co-created the famous Voice Dialogue technique. Prior to meeting Hal, Sidra had begun to study the power of guided imagery. After they met, their mutual interests ignited them to experiment together. As Sidra says, "Hal

> As simple as it sounds, we all must try to be the best person we can: by making the best choices, by making the most of the talents we've been given.
>
> —MARY LOU RETTON, OLYMPIC MEDALIST

and I had been doing guided imagery work with each other and talking about our dreams and exploring one another at some depth. And one day, Hal asked me to move over because he wanted to talk to the child in me—the vulnerable child. And I, being quite sure that I had no such creature within me, moved over and sat down on the floor next to the coffee table and suddenly I was absolutely a preverbal child. I literally moved into the space of a different self, and it was an amazing experience. I was different, the world was different, he was different, and suddenly the door was opened into the magic theater of the selves. Hal was with my child for about an hour. When I went back to the place where I'd originally sat, I was a changed woman. And we both realized that we had seen an amazing event."

This discovery required the dynamics of an intimate relationship. Sidra clearly states, "My creativity has been so entwined with the relationship and his, too. We started seeing not only how the selves acted in and of themselves but we started seeing how they interacted in relationships. Once we got married, we saw how the selves went into these bonding patterns. Those interactions brought us to a whole other level of work." While Sidra wrote *The Shadow King* on her own, she added that Hal was her coach and that she also had the support of Shakti Gawain and company.

When I wrote to interior designer Chris Madden requesting an interview, I got a lovely fax back from her husband Kevin, saying "Yes." Kevin is now her full-time business partner as Chris takes her design knowledge to new and exciting heights. As Chris says, "My gift in life is this man whom I've been with for twenty-eight years. He's the one who has allowed me to take the risks and fly. And it's been that way since I've known him." Kevin was an executive in the magazine business for thirty years, then left that business three years ago to become her partner and more. Chris says, "My incredible husband, who was a corporate warrior, works with me and also runs the house. He keeps everybody going." Chris Madden, Inc., is now made up of six companies that include her books, magazine and newspaper columns, television shows, design services, lectures and seminars, and a new line of furniture. Chris is also a regular on both *Oprah!* and the *Today Show*. Like Sarah

Ban Breathnach, Chris had accomplished much in her lifetime before she became well known and prosperous, but it was her connection to Oprah that changed her life. Oprah's alliances with women in all fields have opened many doors for them. Her generosity and clout are truly remarkable.

Miriam Nelson also acknowledges the critical role of her husband, a classical violinist, in the writing of her two books and her busy lecturing and publicity schedule that has followed. As Miriam says, "I could not do what I do if it weren't for my husband. He's taken complete time off from his career to watch the kids so I can do my work right now. He's really scaled back." These mutual, egalitarian partnerships have allowed these women to blossom creatively and share their inspirations with others successfully.

Collaborating in the Future

The Internet has connected millions of people instantly in ways that were unheard of just yesterday. I see technology ushering us into a time of unprecedented creativity in terms of relationships between companies, customers, individuals, and resources. Envision the kinds of collaborations you want, and there is probably a network that supports your fantasy. The next decade will be a revolution in terms of connections between people and marketplaces. Carve out a niche for yourself and experiment! You don't have to work alone unless you want to.

I have been a solo entrepreneur since 1982 and am rethinking that model for myself. In fact, I have several friends who have or are publishing books and developing products for women at this time, and I'm proposing a collaboration to share mailing lists, workshops, and marketing ideas. It seems foolish for each of us to compile the same information simultaneously, and besides, working together will be fun! I am confident that my next evolution will involve either enlarging my current business, Creative Success, and/or forming innovative strategic alliances with others in the service of women's creativity.

As women, we all have an opportunity to support each other in multiple ways. We can encourage each other to develop and harvest our creative ideas. We can remind each other of the importance of self-focus. By sharing our business expertise with other women and participating in commercial ventures like purchasing a building or going after investors together, we can promote the financial strength of all women. Also, we can channel our investments into women's enterprises or nonprofit organizations that help women. Women and girls receive a minuscule amount of the donated dollars in this country—we can change that. Most of all, be true to yourself and link up with others only in good faith and sincerity.

SECRET 9

Transcending Rejections and Roadblocks

Mastery of this Secret is essential to your creative success. Believing in your creative process or project and persevering through the trials along the way make all the difference.

 Keys

- Working Out Adversity
- Developing Rejection Resilience
- Being Proactive
- Dedicating Yourself to Excellence
- Conveying Strength Instead of Desperation
- Picking Yourself Up Again

There is nothing impossible that someone, who believes
enough in themselves, cannot conquer.

—C. C. H. POUNDER,
ACTRESS AND JEWELRY DESIGNER

*O*nce, when leading a writer's workshop, Marcia Yudkin
asked the participants what they most wanted to get out
of the program. One woman said, "I want to learn how
not to get rejection slips." Marcia told her that the only way to
avoid rejection slips was to go into another business. It's unrealistic
to think that all your ideas will be well received all the time. The
marketplace is driven by investors with their own agendas. Marcia
recognized something that successful creative women know: Rejection and roadblocks are predictable pitfalls of the creative process.

Putting yourself out there and sharing your work qualifies as
an act of courage and tests your fortitude. Maureen Murdock says
that we have to learn how to deal with judgments by other people: "I think people get discouraged too quickly when someone
says 'No.' People are always going to say 'No.' When I first sent
Spinning Inward into the world, I could have papered my den
with the rejections. It's like Eleanor Roosevelt's description about
being a politician: just grow the skin of a rhinoceros. That's my
best advice to give to women, make a commitment to yourself,
and then grow the skin of a rhinoceros."

Dr. Clarissa Pinkola Estés also encountered rejections prior to
her tremendous success. "I wrote *Women Who Run with the
Wolves* over twenty years' time as part of a larger work of *100
Tales of the Inner Life*. During those twenty years, it was rejected
forty-seven times by small, medium, and large publishing
houses—teaching me that rejection is an equal opportunity un-
employer. During that time I held many jobs, in addition to that
of a healer, in order to support my family and to strive toward my
education. I earnestly and happily—and I hope also artfully—
worked as hairdresser, hash-slinger, PBX operator, rivet-machin-
ist, picker-and-packer, rock painter, newsletter editor for
meatpackers, night-shift bakerwoman, deliverer of phone books,
and more." Yet in the end, victory rewarded her tenacity.

As we all know, rejection can be heartwrenching. It's tempting to take it personally and doubt the rightness of our work or our worth. Creative ideas can be so innovative that the marketplace may not be ready for them or understand their value. Or criticism may be valid. If we can get past the rejection itself and listen to the themes or sentiments being expressed, we can often shift our project toward acceptance.

With the proposal for this book, I learned that writing this as a novel diminished its chances for publication and that formatting a book with a chapter on each person I interviewed made marketing difficult for publishers. I finally heard these realities enough times that I used them and rewrote my proposal for the zillionth time. Fortunately, I received wonderful feedback from women in publishing who liked my idea, and I was confident that women needed inspiration and information on the creative process. My mission was to get this "portable mentor" out to women, so I had to either coordinate my vision with the needs of publishers or self-publish. It didn't feel like a compromise; I chose to partner with Conari Press so that this book would reach more women, and because I'm aligned with their mission to publish books that make a difference.

Challenge: ACCEPTANCE FANTASIES

List ten fantasies about where you would like your work to be accepted, seen, or purchased. Describe these fantasies in great detail, including how you make the connection, what you are wearing, which work is involved, how well you handle the negotiations, and how much you get either paid or rewarded for your efforts.

> When you want something, go back and go back and go back, and don't take "No" for an answer. And when rejection comes, don't take it personally. It goes with the territory. Expose yourself to as much humiliation as you can bear, then go home and go do it all again tomorrow.
>
> —BETTY FURNESS, ACTIVIST AND WRITER

Working Out Adversity

Managing rejections divides us into two camps: those who stop after one or two rejections, and those who maintain their convictions and keep going, accumulating even more rejections. As any experienced salesperson knows, every rejection leads you closer to a sale. In addition to just deciding to hang in there, be strategic about how to get what you want. As women, we may be so wired up to please others and seek approval that inviting rejection truly tests our belief in ourselves.

It also means encountering and countering competition. Analyzing the competition and the uniqueness of your project comprises a critical component of any creative proposal.

Few people experience instantaneous success, or if they do, it may not last. Knowing when to hang in there and when to comprise is often a psychologically and financially challenging dilemma. Every creative specialty has its protocol, and it's wise to learn the rules before you plunge in. This is where support from others can be invaluable.

Criticism has to be evaluated—can we learn from it or is it off target and useless? It's hard to know at first. For writer Carol Frenier, a painful rejection led her to a beneficial revision of her work. When Carol began sending out query letters to publishers for her book, she got varied responses. One publisher was most enthusiastic and asked to see the manuscript, which was then 120 pages. The editor then called Carol to say that she read it all the way through without falling asleep, which was unusual, and thought it was great. They had a wonderful conversation, and she told Carol that she would meet with her editorial committee and let her know in a few months. Since Carol is an experienced president for a marketing company, she was cautious but very excited.

Then, remembers Carol, "When she called back in late September, my husband and I were probably at the worst point in our business. Everything was falling apart and we had a big client who went bankrupt, leaving us with a major receivable of $37,000. The market was flat. The possibility of publishing this book was the one bright light. But the editor called back and said that they had turned it down as they wanted a more focused book for businesswomen. I was just blown away. I was devastated. I went out and sat in the garden and just sobbed my brains out. I just let myself sink into it and didn't try to edit my response at all."

Carol has a quiet inner strength of immense power. She has studied Jung and the potency of dreams for many years and

> Being defeated is often a temporary condition. Giving up is what makes it permanent.
> —Marilyn vos Savant, writer

connects moment to moment with her spiritual wisdom. Carol took her grief to bed and woke up the next morning with a vision: "I don't know what I dreamt, but I woke up with the whole book reconfigured. The image of the phoenix rising is the one most powerful in my mind, because it was really like that." With her husband away on a business trip for ten days, Carol wrote nine hours a day until she was "brain dead." Then she sent the new version of her manuscript back out to publishers. Shortly after, she got a call from the gifted publishing director at Butterworth-Heinemann, Karen Speerstra, who was very excited by Carol's concept and agreed to publish the book.

Barbara Sher, the fairy godmother of career counseling, exemplifies the value of believing in your work and holding on. Her first book, *Wishcraft,* which has been an all-time bestseller, was almost buried. So Barbara went to the publisher and asked to buy it back. This shocked the publisher so much that they issued short runs every now and then, until finally it became an underground hit. Barbara's persistence was the result of an educated guess—she knew from the letters she received from readers, the feedback from clients, and the enormous response from her workshop participants that the book effectively helped people.

Barbara's second book *Teamworks* went out of print, but she sought out a new agent and tried again. She has since written several more wonderful books, created audiotape programs, and received tremendous publicity. By staying committed to her work, she created her own Success Team: "My Success Team is my wonderful publisher, my talented agent, and my partner in California who produces my tapes."

These folks believe in Barbara and promote her. For both Carol and Barbara, perseverance and discovering the right formula to support their work led them to success. They used their roadblocks to move them toward better choices.

Philosophically, Barbara Waugh, agent of change extraordinaire, doesn't believe in roadblocks. Barbara has fought many battles for women and minorities, including her two adopted African American children, as well as for revolutionary personnel practices in the worldwide Hewlett-Packard Labs community. She says, "I

> You may have to fight a battle more than once to win it.
> —MARGARET THATCHER, FORMER PRIME MINISTER OF ENGLAND

> When you come to a roadblock, take a detour.
> —MARY KAY ASH, ENTREPRENEUR

think a roadblock is a signpost instead of a barrier. Maybe it's telling you something. If so, what? I know you run up against things. I'm not real mystical about this—I think it's eminently practical. You will have a better life, feel happier and more empowered to do what you want to do, if you frame it that a roadblock is really an indicator. Frame it so that the person who is against you is actually holding a truth that is valuable for your path, and you'll have more wins."

Barbara's comment reminded me of Awiakta's story, one which many Cherokee mothers teach their daughters and sons: "The secrets of the true warrior are persistence, courage, and psyching your adversary. In modern terms, that means psyching the system—you have to understand what you're up against." To engage with our adversaries, we have to disconnect our societal scripts, which taught us women to always be nice, agreeable, and seek approval. Accessing the power of your inner warrior is essential to handling rebuffs and to rerouting criticism.

Challenge: COMMEMORATING YOUR WARRIOR VICTORIES

When you are struggling with an adversary or a disappointment, recall those times in your life when you fought for something and won. That is your warrior energy. You might even want to make a warrior memorial for yourself commemorating those life victories in words, pictures, or symbols. Use your memorial to help you fuel your inner strength when you feel vulnerable.

Developing Rejection Resilience

To be tested is good. The challenged life may be the best therapist.
—GAIL SHEEHY, WRITER

As creative women, one of the other skills we need to develop is Rejection Resilience. We must be able to move in the world knowing that not everyone will approve of us or our creative accomplishments consistently.

I once heard a great story about several women writers who feared rejection but wanted to get their work published. So they formed a collective and sent each other's work out to publishers. They each followed up on the other person's work, handled the rejections, and kept sending out for each other. It worked, and they each eventually got published and felt less bruised by the process. If the outside support is not possible, we need to learn to prop ourselves up, which requires practice and perseverance. As an old expression says, "No one can intimidate you without your permission." By knowing your vulnerable hot spots, you are better prepared to protect yourself because you can sort out the valuable information that helps you find the right home for your work.

You also need to do a psychological check on how prepared you are to face rejection. Most of us need a support system to depend on when we encounter negativity and disappointment.

If you have unresolved traumas, then be especially careful to structure a top-notch team of allies for yourself, and take the necessary time to build up your Rejection Resilience. To assess the help you might need, take a few minutes to fill out this inventory.

Challenge: YOUR REJECTION VULNERABILITY

1. Think back over your life and make a list of all of the times you have felt rejected for yourself and/or your work. Who rejected you and/or your work and why? How did he/she/they do it? Were you attacked as a person, ignored, or given constructive/destructive feedback on your project? How emotionally traumatic were those experiences for you? Have you healed from those rejections? Do you still need to resolve them before you venture into a new arena where you will most likely be criticized or rejected by someone?

2. In regard to your creative work, what are you most insecure about? As a person, what are you most insecure about? Sum up your vulnerabilities by completing these two sentences:

Getting ahead in a difficult profession—singing, acting, writing, whatever—requires avid faith in yourself. You must be able to sustain yourself against staggering blows and unfair reversals. When I think back to those first couple of years in Rome, those endless rejections, without a glimmer of encouragement from anyone, all those failed screen tests, and yet I never let my desire slide away from me, my belief in myself and what I felt I could achieve.

—SOPHIA LOREN, ACTRESS

In regard to my work, I am most afraid of being criticized or rejected for... As a person, I am most afraid of being criticized or rejected for...

3. In your experiences promoting your work or yourself, what are the specific comments or objections you have encountered from people who have rejected your work? Are they fair comments? Is there truth in them? Do you have a weakness that needs to be remedied? Keep a rejection file and sort through it from time to time to note any patterns. What does this particular marketplace want from you? Are you interested in or willing to coordinate your work with that message?

Being Proactive

One of my favorite stories of bravado comes from illustrator Jan Brett. Jan is an avid horsewoman and also learned to fly a plane solo. Mastering flying solo greatly boosted her faith in herself.

As Jan says, "When I flew, it was about the same time that I really pushed my work by trying to get into editors' offices to get jobs and projects. The flying helped my self-confidence. After I had soloed, I'd come home and tell myself, 'Well, if I can solo, then I can certainly call these editors,' and I did."

Many people find that tackling great physical challenges like rock climbing or ropes courses bolsters their strength. When you are facing new frontiers with your work, recall life experiences where you felt powerful and competent. Think about activities that boost your self-esteem, and leverage them during times when you are stretching your safety zone. Identify the skills you used to overcome obstacles and apply them to your creative endeavor. Keep challenging yourself to build your self-confidence. Find a buddy and try new activities on a regular basis.

Dedicating Yourself to Excellence

Restaurateur Lydia Shire also has a success strategy worth noting. After her marriage broke up, Lydia made the decision to become a

> You've got to take the initiative and play your game.... Confidence makes the difference.
> —CHRIS EVERETT, TENNIS PRO

chef, and began her career as a salad girl in the early '70s. As usual, she maximized her potential: "I knew then that in order to get ahead, you had to be the best in the whole crew. So I understood early on that it would require me spending my own money to go to France or visit great restaurants in New York to learn. A lot of people don't realize that you have to invest in your own future. I think far too many people just spend eight hours at work and assume that they've done all they had to do. But I would go in early and make specials, and at night I'd go home and read cookbooks, which really helped me. Back then, I never asked anybody for a raise, I was always just given them."

Lydia's excellence paid off as she worked her way up to become the chef of the renowned French restaurant Maison Robert in Boston—quite a feat for an American woman. It was there that Julia Child discovered Lydia's talent. When you eat at Lydia's two extraordinary restaurants today, her commitment to quality impresses you with every bite. It's easy to understand why she and her partner Susan Regis are revered as the best chefs in Boston. As Lydia's experiences show, becoming truly outstanding at your chosen creative endeavor gives you a critical edge in the rejection game. First of all, you will most likely be rejected less often, and second, if you can stand behind your own work knowing you tried your best, rejection's sting will not detour you for long.

> I was taught that the way of progress is neither swift nor easy.
> —MARIE CURIE, PHYSICIST AND CHEMIST

Challenge: ACHIEVING EXCELLENCE

Critically evaluate what you ought to do in order for your acceptance fantasies to come true. Do you need more paintings, cleverer designs, a published book, a snappier workshop, some public relations, a review by someone famous, a makeover, better connections, sales skills, business skills, capital, a new idea or direction? Be as specific as possible about what you're missing, so you can clearly determine what's stopping those fantasies from happening. Make a list of your missing ingredients and get to work on them.

Conveying Strength Instead of Desperation

Believing in yourself and your work will help you resist the desperation trap. As C. C. H. Pounder notes, there are some behaviors that actually invite rejection. As an actress, she has a tremendous amount of knowledge about perception: "People can smell hungry. I don't know how they do it, but hunger is a very, very potent smell. I had a friend who is a perfectly capable good actor but very, very hungry. She went for a reading and I asked her how it went and she said, 'It was great. I had a great time.' I asked her what time she left. She said, 'Oh, well, you know, as I was leaving, I just stopped at the secretary's desk to see who else was on the list and then we chatted about something else. Then I had a glass of water and went to the bathroom and just popped back in to leave a few extra resumes.' And I said, 'You lost the job.' She said, 'Why?' I said, 'If you're satisfied with what you've done and you can walk away with assurance, then all they have to remember is the work you did in that room. You have to keep that mystery going, of, wow, that person just whipped in here, did that, and she's gone. That spells confidence.'" C. C. H. was right—her friend didn't get the part.

Actress Christina Pickles echoes C. C. H.'s sentiments: "Producers are so afraid that they don't want to hire somebody who's afraid. So if you show fear, it triggers their own fear because there's so much money riding on everything."

Desperation is familiar territory for most of us at some point in our lives, but people tend to recoil from it. So if we telegraph that we'll do or take anything, our work may be less valued by others. As C. C. H. says, if we show people that we have no place else to go, they may think twice about wanting us.

Desperation is also dangerous for another reason. Not only could we get ourselves and our work rejected if we're too eager, we often don't make wise decisions because of our lust for results. I can't tell you the number of clients I have seen over the past two decades who chose bad partners or accepted poorly defined jobs at terrible companies because they devalued their abilities and didn't cultivate enough options for themselves. Before you align yourself with a potential client, customer, or organization, do a desperation check on yourself.

Challenge: Are You Desperate?

Ask yourself the following questions: Do I want this acceptance too much? What are the other alternatives? What are the indicators that this is a good or bad alliance? What is my intuition saying about this person or place? What is my value to them? Am I selling myself short?

> You may be disappointed if you fail, but you are doomed if you don't try.
> —Beverly Sills,
> opera singer

Instead of focusing exclusively on whether or not a potential client or customer accepts you, ask yourself whether or not they meet *your* standards.

Picking Yourself Up Again

Is it worth it to sustain an agonizing situation for future gain? Sometimes, yes. Maureen Murdock had a bad experience with one publisher and almost lost her confidence as a writer. The publisher's lack of respect and support was disastrous. "There was no respect for the writer," she remembers. "I was treated lower than any janitor in any public lavatory in any public city. I was shattered emotionally. It was the most abusive situation I've ever been in in my life. And the thing that was most upsetting was that it was at the hands of a woman." For a year after, she wrote about "meandering" as she tried to restore her health and her voice, and she finally did. Maureen recaptured her faith in herself and now has a positive relationship with the publisher Shambhala, where her editor, Emily Sell, has been an extraordinary support.

Jewel, a client of mine who is a manufacturer's representative for an Italian furniture line she discovered on a trip abroad, took on a sales associate to help her implement an innovative marketing plan. Three months later, Jewel discovered that this associate had made her own deals with prospects, stealing a substantial percentage of Jewel's business. Because Jewel had never set up a contractual agreement between them, it was difficult for her to recoup her losses. In addition to losing business, Jewel now had legal bills to fund as well.

It turns out that Jewel had not thoroughly checked this associate's background, and discovered her history of shady dealings the hard way. Forgiving herself for these oversights was the hardest thing for Jewel. Whenever we take risks, sometimes they flop. Jewel learned a valuable lesson about impatience, implemented a damage control plan, and eventually hired a talented and ethical new associate.

As little girls, we had to learn to pick ourselves up after a fall, get first aid for our scrapes, and then venture back outside to play. Recovery and reentry are also crucial skills for creative women. The world often knocks us down, and we wear the scars to signify the blows. We have to choose whether to retreat or retry. So many of the women in this book decided to reemerge from collisions with adversity. Remember their stories when you feel like you're all alone out there and want to hide out in your safety zone. Too many women get rejected once or twice and lock their creativity up in a closet forever. We all lose as a result.

Challenge: SECURING YOUR MISSING INGREDIENTS

Locate people who have accomplished what you want to and try to meet them, read about them, or study their work. Try to figure out the secrets of their success. Cross-check what you learn from this exercise with your own list of missing ingredients from the previous exercise. Did these role models have your missing ingredients? Which ones? Put a star next to the missing ingredients that are most important. Are you willing to take the risks necessary to add those ingredients to your portfolio? If so, make a plan for yourself with goals for the next year, maximum. Are there missing ingredients that you are unwilling to commit to—for example, having a face lift, becoming a public speaker, doing art you don't like? If so, are any of these

> Life's ups and downs provide windows of opportunity to determine your values and goals. Think of using all obstacles as stepping stones to build the life you want.
> —MARSHA SINETAR, AUTHOR

missing ingredients truly essential to your success? If you're not going to do them, can someone else handle that part of your business? If it is clear that you are not going to strive for achieving certain of the missing ingredients, then devise ways to work around them. We each have to be true to ourselves first.

Third Gateway

Actualizing Creative Results:
The Power of Positive Priorities

I don't want life to imitate art.
I want life to be art.

—CARRIE FISHER, ACTRESS

Living in Abundance with Positive Priorities

You can design a life of creative fulfillment for yourself. You have the opportunity to select your goals for an abundant life of positive choices to enhance your creativity.

Keys

- Defining Abundance
- Tapping into the Power of Gratitude
- Doing What You Love
- Caring for Your Body and Mind
- Knowing What Supports and Detracts from Your Creativity
- Identifying Your Personal Positive Priorities

The creative process gives back tenfold.
It is by definition abundant and unending.

—CATHLEEN ROUNTREE, ARTIST AND WRITER

*A*bundance is the experience of plenty, often called prosperity. In her book, *Open Your Mind to Prosperity,* my first prosperity mentor, Catherine Ponder, says, "You are prosperous to the degree that you are experiencing peace, health, and plenty in your world." Shakti Gawain says in her book *Creating True Prosperity* that prosperity is "the experience of having plenty of what we truly need and want in life, material and otherwise." For creative women, the opportunity to dance with the creative process is itself an experience of abundance. In our culture however, abundance is often equated only with money, the pursuit of which may throw our body, mind, and spirit out of balance, and therefore threaten our creative flow.

When we are in touch with true abundance, it permeates the fabric of our lives. It includes passion, both romantic and creative; positive relationships with people, animals, and nature; life experiences you crave and enjoy; personal and professional challenges and growth; and individual moments to savor. Abundance invites us to live the life we desire instead of settling for less. Having our basic physical and shelter needs met certainly forms a key foundation, but beyond the basics, there are a multitude of life choices to be made. In order to tap into our creativity and enjoy a sense of abundance, we need to make certain choices, choices that may require sacrifices.

Defining Abundance

Designer Joanne Rossman says, "I'm a bajillionairess in friends and experiences. From early on, I had friends whose families had maids and chauffeured cars, and I just thought that was fabulous. I have clients who fly me in their Lear jets and invite me to stay on Park Avenue. I've always been able to mix with the moneyed people and not feel embarrassed or uncomfortable. But my history is not about making money or having money. There is no question that I could make more money if I were better financed—if I had a stronger cash flow going. I am also completely aware that I won't compromise a lot of things." Joanne is quite open about the fact that she wants her scarves to be hand-done, doesn't like to be pushed, and prefers to work at her own pace. If that means making less money, that's okay with her.

Despite our best intentions, it is not unusual to have a crisis of faith at times and get trapped in "scarcity thinking." The voice of scarcity thinking is another saboteur of sorts. It is the voice of "not having enough" or "being at risk." It worships lack rather than plenty. Scarcity thinking comes from fear and a lack of trust that your needs will be taken care of.

Cathleen Rountree told me she had a close encounter with scarcity thinking when she learned that her charming little book *Fifty Ways to Meet Your Lover* was due to go out of print. For Cathleen, this setback served to remind her of all of the talents she could leverage to support herself if necessary, including becoming a dog walker in Manhattan because, as she explains with a laugh, "I say hello to every dog I ever meet and I'd be good at it." While money has historically been an issue for Cathleen, she exudes abundance and says, "I enjoy my life. I just feel enormously grateful. Every day I do what I want to, which comes from self-knowledge and commitment. I have a vision of what's important to me and how to accomplish that. I want to live my authenticity with grace and beauty. I feel better going for the adventure than holding myself back out of fear. That would be death already." Cathleen's eyes glow when she talks about her many loves—photography, writing, painting, and film—and it is clear that she will never run out of art forms to play with. Her house is filled with beautiful things and she surrounds herself with flowers. For balance, Cathleen finds that the contrast between her quiet life in California and her quarterly visits to visit her son in New York, complete with its innumerable films, plays, museums, and meetings, suits her. Her sanctuary in California allows her to sink into her creative process, accompanied by her dog Sienna. Cathleen is now ready for a partner to complement her already abundant life, but this partner has to celebrate her creativity, not compete with it.

> Life's challenges are not supposed to paralyze you, they're supposed to help you discover who you are.
> —BERNICE JOHNSON REAGON, MUSICIAN

Creative freedom is the backbone of prosperity for me and for many of the women profiled in this book. This lifestyle values quality of living more than the pursuit of security. Many daring women refuse to follow a path they know does not suit them. Knowing yourself, believing in your inspirations, and making the tough choices to follow your inner knowing necessitates fortitude.

Indeed, a life of Positive Priorities—life choices that express who we are and what we want for ourselves—is in itself a creative act. Each of us has a different spin on it. Our decisions about life choices determine our personal equilibrium with abundance, including money, security, and balance. All of the great prosperity teachers ask the same question about money: How much money is really enough? Enough for what? The illusion of security too often seduces people away from self-expression and fulfillment. Many wealthy people never experience their own prosperity, for wealth carries its own fears, just like poverty. Abundance beckons as a state of mind, beginning with gratitude for what you already have and followed by a vision of what you want to create in your life. Prosperity consciousness demands that you look beyond the energy of money and own up to what it is that truly nourishes you. Of the women I interviewed, some have earned millions with their creative energies while others live within great financial constraints. Yet, all have lives abundant with excitement, energy, commitment, adventure, and personal growth.

Engaging with your creative self is a joy unto itself. Painting a vision on a canvas has its own special reward. The question of whether or not it sells is a different issue. The glory of bringing that painting into existence in the first place is what truly matters. Creativity has its own payoff, and we each choose whether or not we want to make a business out of our revelations.

> One of the secrets of a happy life is continuous small treats.
>
> —IRIS MURDOCH, WRITER

> Life is change. Growth is optional. Choose wisely.
>
> —KAREN KAISER CLARK, WRITER

Challenge: YOUR PERSONAL ABUNDANCE

Take a few moments and write a paragraph about what abundance means for you in your life. What kind of life would be ideal for you? What Positive Priorities would support that vision? Who/what are your most precious possessions, relationships, and experiences? Are you living your life according to what's most valuable to you? If not, what needs to change? How are you using your gift of time? How do abundance and balance interplay with each other in your daily and ongoing decisions? What underlying values are reflected in your experience of living? What sparks your creative power? Write a summary statement of your answers.

Tapping into the Power of Gratitude

More than fifteen years ago, I took my first prosperity class with a Unity minister and learned about the power of gratitude. Our first homework assignment was to make a list of everything in our lives that we were grateful for. I remember feeling astonished at the length of my first gratitude list and how many blessings I took for granted. As relationships, personal growth, books, and vacations emerged as key blessings for me, it put many things into perspective. The power of this exercise changes your worldview and teaches you to appreciate the richness of moments and the offerings available to you each day if you stop to notice. Sarah Ban Breathnach, in her book *The Simple Abundance Journal of Gratitude,* has widely publicized this practice and says, "Gratitude is the most passionate transformative power in the cosmos. When we offer thanks to God or to another human being, gratitude gifts us with renewal, reflection, reconnection." Her instructions are to write down five things that you are grateful for every day. Some days this task is easier than others, but the mindset consistently creates perspective and thankfulness.

Many of the women profiled in this book have proactively designed a life of Positive Priorities for which they are most grateful. To be fully creative, you must notice what fuels your creative energy and what drains it, and map out your life accordingly. Dancer Leslie Neal exudes gratitude for her blessings when she says, "I have abundance in my life, but it doesn't have anything to do with money, although I've been well supported. But I've also been clear on some funny level about not wanting my art to be my

Prosperity is having the power to create a life of your choice— to get what you really want, not just what you're handed.
—RUTH ROSS,
WRITER

source of income, which has kept me from asking too much from it. I've always been grateful that it didn't have to. Talk about gratitude, I've always been given exactly what I need by listening to my inner voice and following it! Teaching dance at the university allows me to use my skills as a dance teacher and artist and earn a living doing what I love."

Challenge: IDENTIFYING SCARCITY THINKING

What kinds of anti-prosperity messages or scarcity thoughts does your fearful mind resort to? What triggers distrust and negativity for you? What is the source of your scarcity thinking—family, society, personal experience, lack of spiritual beliefs? What helps you to calm your fears? What evidence is there in your life that the universe will take care of you? What practical measures can you take to augment your prosperity consciousness?

Doing What You Love

Stress is a creativity killer. The secret to living in abundance is learning the art of making positive life choices. Fifteen years ago when I was on the road teaching stress management seminars, I developed this important theory.

While meditations, exercise, and vacations all have the potential to reduce negative stress, you can lie on the floor all you want and relax, but if your relationships are lousy or you hate your work or your creativity is being stifled, you will remain stressed out. Your life choices, positive and negative, determine your well-being. Negative life choices steal your peace of mind and compromise your potential as a creative conduit. True Positive Priorities living means productively resolving the problems in your life and activating life choices such as living where you want, doing work you love, surrounding yourself with mutually fulfilling relationships, and taking care of your mind, body, and spirit. By learning the art of making positive life choices, you can resolve the stressful challenges in your life and free your creative energy.

Live with no
time out.
—SIMONE DE BEAUVOIR,
WRITER

Writing coach Marcia Yudkin, for example, chooses not to do unappealing business writing and says, "Business writing is more lucrative than just working with writers, but there are certain kinds of business writing I know I would hate. It'd be a kind of slavery to me and life is too short." When I asked Marcia how she manages stress and keeps her life in balance, she also had an enlightening reply: "It's not that hard because I enjoy what I do. So it's not like I'm doing something terrible and I then have to balance it with something that I like. Except for brief periods when I have a deadline and things get kind of frantic, my time's my own. Most of the time I get to do what I want."

Loving your creative work eliminates a lot of stress and strain and the need for what I call "work anti-dotes," which are things you need to do to recover from work that poisons your soul. We've all had jobs like that, with insane bosses, too many rules, or no options to participate in the decisions that impact our work lives. These kinds of inhumane workplaces steal our lives away. Most of the women in this book have been unwilling to work in these kinds of organizations and instead choose to purify their relationship with work, their creativity, and themselves.

Photographer Alison Shaw made a great comment about creative work and clock watching. Now that she gets to photograph what beckons to her, she finds that her days aren't long enough: "My whole relationship with the clock and the calendar, in terms of work, is wanting more time. I look at the clock and feel stunned that it's 5 o'clock when I wish it was only 1 o'clock. I choose to feel that way about my work."

In my days as a management consultant and trainer, I heard many horror stories about unhealthy workplaces. In fact, when I would go into a company to run a Positive Priorities workshop, in just a few hours, I could tell you what was wrong with the place. It became obvious, for example, that the managers hadn't been trained, no one communicated honestly, or that people were unappreciated. These dysfunctional work environments undermine people's creative spirits and their joy of living. But, by building a life of Positive Priorities, you can more easily manifest your creative goals.

> There is no shortage of good days. It is good lives that are hard to come by.
> —ANNIE DILLARD, WRITER

Challenge: YOUR LIFE ENHANCERS

Write down ten things you'd really like to do in your life. Don't censor—just write. The context of your life is a creativity enhancer itself. Look over your list. What is stopping you from experiencing these dreams now? No one else can grant you a fulfilling life. You are the author of your own story. Is it an adventure story or a tragedy? You can redirect the plot at any time. By ensuring that you add these ten life-enhancing Positive Priorities to your life experience as soon as possible, your tale will have a happier ending. Commit to these ten goals and set up a timeline with target dates and action steps. No one else can do this for you.

Use your life enhancers as a starting point to turn your life into a creative work of art. For example, just by adding in a week at a health spa every year, Suzanne, a successful entrepreneur, felt much more in control of her destiny. This year she relishes experiencing another one of her life enhancers through building a greenhouse in her backyard to cultivate organic vegetables.

> Instead of thinking about where you are, think about where you want to be. It takes twenty years of hard work to become an overnight success.
>
> —DIANA RANKIN, WRITER

Caring for Your Body and Mind

Self-management is also an important category of Positive Priorities. Let's start with the physical body. Caring for our physical body creates a foundation for health and well-being, but it also has other benefits as well. The entertainer Madonna discovered Ashtanga yoga when she was seven months pregnant with her daughter and claims it has changed her life. She outgrew the intensity of the gym and sank into the lessons of yoga. In an interview in the *Boston Globe,* she comments, "It was the hardest thing I've ever done, but it was really focused and there was a great simplicity as well. I'm a total perfectionist who beats up on myself when I don't get things right. And so I had to learn to (a) not judge myself; and (b) to let go of the idea that I had to accomplish this and master it in one day. So it taught me patience and judgment. Now I feel that yoga is a total metaphor for life. If you're in a hurry, you can't embrace or enjoy yoga. So that was another lesson for me—to enjoy the stillness of it."

Tall and lithe, Leslie Neal believes she was born to dance. She is also profoundly insightful about the power of movement in the process of self-development: "I think we are all inherently movers and dancers. We were born to move; movement is life! The very first awareness our mothers have of us in the womb is movement—that's how we're first recognized as being alive."

Leslie says that dancing keeps her grounded and fuels her spiritual and creative selves as well. She also claims, "Everything I know spiritually I have learned through body awareness. It is how I 'move' through my world."

Challenge: YOU AND YOUR BODY

Take a moment to think about how you feel about your body—this vessel that you walk around in. Do you feel healthy? Are you grounded? Are you in touch with your physical being? Can you acknowledge the glory of your physical body or are you fixated on its imperfections? Close your eyes briefly and ask your body what it needs from you. Note the conversation and remember your body's wisdom. How does your body assist your creative self? Is there a way to fortify your body to support your creative energies? What changes do you need to make in your life to enhance the strength and well-being of your physical support system? Keep track of your ideas.

Yes, I'm fifty-three years old, but I don't think about it. I only think of what I must do tomorrow—that I must dance Swan Lake, that I must dance Sleeping Beauty.
—MARGOT FONTEYN, DANCER

For women in American culture, thin is in. But thin can be very dangerous to your health and your self-esteem. Thin is also often temporary; it may vanish with youth. Yet, the models in the magazines and the stunning women on television are very thin. I once read that many models eat baby food instead of real food to stay so svelte. All of us have our own relationships with genes, metabolism, and aging, and to have one standard for all women is absurdly damaging. This anorexic standard causes many women to reject or neglect communications with their physical bodies, which is unhealthy on many levels. It is a question of power for all women, as Awiakta identifies so astutely in *Selu,* through her poem called "Anorexia Bulimia Speaks from the Grave," written for Judy (1966–1992).

Anorexia Bulimia Speaks from the Grave
Young women, listen to me—
I'm talkin' to you.
Don't come down here before your time.
It's dark and cold.
Nothin' doin' down here.
but the Grandmothers sayin'

'Anorexia Bulimia!
Tell the young women this for us:
They bound our feet
and our toes busted out—
to travel on, test new waters.
They bound our breasts...
our nipples busted out,
infra-red eyes to take in
what the other two miss.
When they bound our middle
rib 'n hip busted the stays
     took the waist with 'em—
     free as they were born.

But now, young women—*now*...
They've got your soul in a bind,
wounded, wound up
in electronic wire and hard paper twine
that cuts images into your brain,

unnatural images sayin'
'Starve yourself to suit us.
Starve your body.
Starve your power.
Starve your dream—
thinner and thinner—
until YOU vanish.'

They want you to do that
'cause if you was to take on weight
you might start throwin' it around.
No way can They handle
a full-grown woman
with a full-grown dream. No way.

Listen young women,
the Grandmothers and Anorexia Bulimia
are talkin' to you—
Feed your body.
Feed your soul.
Feed your dream.
BUST OUT!!!

If we women honor and cherish our physical bodies, we can be in our power. Devaluing ourselves for not being thin or not mirroring society's standards of how our physical body should look can silence our creative voices. As Awiakta says, it may keep you quiet and passive so that you don't affirm yourself and your talents. This world needs women who will speak their truth and actively participate. I was saddened to read a comment by Cher in the "Star Bio's" Web site that says, "I'm insecure about everything, because . . . I'm never going to look in the mirror and see this blond, blue-eyed girl. That is my idea of what I'd like to look like." Cher is an extraordinary actress, so this comment undermines her self-worth. I'd love to be taller myself and go back to my college weight, but we all have to learn to live with our limitations. The question is, as women, how much does insecurity about your imperfect body limit your creative courage?

Leslie Neal believes strongly that "what cuts women off from their empowerment is the cultural idea that our bodies are a shamed place rather than a source of beauty, creativity, and strength. As women, we need to find pride in our physicalness and trust our internal knowledge. Body, mind, and spirit—it's all connected. What I try to do most with my students is get them back to their bodies, into the consciousness of the wisdom of their bodies and how good it feels to move and not be restricted by some kind of antiquated belief that you're not allowed to revel and rejoice in that exhilaration." Movement is a positive choice; it supports a healthy body, releases pain, and frees the spirit. Almost every one of the women profiled in this book exercised regularly. Energy fuels creativity.

Knowing What Supports and Detracts from Your Creativity

Self-knowledge helps you to select choices for the lifestyle that suits you. For example, for some women, having children is a positive choice, while for others, like businesswoman and social worker Joline Godfrey, it's not: "I never had a second in my life, ever, that I wanted children. I couldn't be doing what I'm doing, frankly, if I had children of my own." While Joline is spearheading a movement that benefits young girls, parenting her own children is not what she wants for herself. For both singer Rebecca Parris and activist Barbara Waugh, adopting children has brought them great fulfillment.

We all have to find the formula that's right for us. Shakti Gawain has made a conscious decision to travel less to do workshops and instead work more intensively with groups of people at her beautiful retreat in Kauai. She has also just reorganized her publishing business so she can focus more on the creative side. Guiding principles for her life choices include "being able to say 'No' to things that don't feel wonderful" and "trying to work less and nurture myself more."

Ceramist Rosette Gault says that the most important key for getting creative is being grounded, so she uses meditation,

Buddhist chanting, and tai chi as practices to enhance her process. "As a creative person, it helps me to have a routine daily life—regular meal times and a regular schedule. That's why I was so productive at Banff Center for the Arts; I lived in a structure, and was free, at least temporarily, of money and domestic worries."

For writer Maureen Murdock, teaching is an essential choice for her since it ignites her creative inspirations. "My writing is very much gathered from my work with people. I'm an experiential learner and an experiential teacher, so I think my writing, in a sense, is reportage on my understanding of what's going on with people, both in my practice and in the community. I try to pick up the pulse of our generation."

> We all live in suspense from day to day; in other words, you are the hero of your own story.
> —Mary McCarthy, writer

Identifying Your Personal Positive Priorities

In order for you to maximize your creative potential, you first have to figure out what you want. Only you can discover the right abundance formula that works for you. The women interviewed for this book highlighted the following list of Positive Priorities:

1. Time for creative exploration
2. Fulfilling work
3. Encouraging partners, friends, and community
4. Personal growth experiences, such as psychotherapy, body work, workshops
5. Good health, including nutrition, meditation, and exercise
6. Nurturing living spaces
7. Continued learning opportunities
8. Self-protection from negativity and toxic people
9. Reflective time such as vacations, health spas, and retreats
10. Spiritual practices and beliefs that support their process
11. Independence in action and thought
12. Solitude as needed
13. Inner security and centeredness
14. Connection with nature and the arts

15. Activities that stimulate inspiration

16. Balance

Think about what Positive Priorities you'd like to add to your life, set aside at least an hour of quiet time, and visualize a lifetime of new goals with this excercise:

Challenge: POSITIVE PRIORITIES VISUALIZATION

(Note: You may want to record this exercise on audiotape or have a trusted friend read it to you very slowly to get its full benefit.)

Find a quiet place where you will be undisturbed. Get comfortable, close your eyes, and relax. Imagine your body melting into marshmallow fluff. Just let go and listen to your thoughts and feelings as they float through your mind. Imagine doing wonderful creative work you love, having peak experiences in your life, living out your goals, and relishing simply being. Picture yourself in mutual loving relationships, having fun with friends, living in your dream house, and enjoying the days of your life. Imagine feeling a balance between peacefulness and the excitement of new challenges and learning. Assume that the right amount of money is available to you. Let your fantasies speak to you. All your negatives are gone, so you have a blank screen on which to create the life you were meant to live. Notice any limiting beliefs that tell you that you can't have what you want and let them vanish. Keep visualizing the essence of what you wish to initiate in your life. When the ideas stop flowing, come back to the present, and write down all of the Positive Priorities you can remember. Preserve the ideas that you have captured in your notebook.

Repeat this exercise regularly to update your desires. Over time, by adding your personal Positive Priorities, one at a time, your life experience will move closer to your vision. Each step forward is a catalyst for refinement.

Your selection of Positive Priorities is the foundation for your life path and your creative expression, invented by you, reflective of your uniqueness. To make your goals more visual, try the following challenge:

Challenge: POSITIVE PRIORITIES ROAD MAP

In your notebook, draw a picture of a road and divide the road of your life into two-year blocks. In each block, write down what you want manifest in your life during that time, using your Positive Priorities list as a guide. You may want to add a visual perspective with drawings or pictures from magazines to highlight each concept.

Tatiana, a client of mine, wanted to go back to school in interior design and specialize in creating magnificent kitchens for cooking couples. In order to achieve this goal, she had to release her fears about academia and create a financial plan to support her overhead. She identified several Positive Priorities, like working at a design school to cut her tuition, taking care of children, which she loves, and bartering with a mentor to smooth her ride. Tatiana wanted the overall experience to be wonderful, not taxing.

Plot out your own passage now and update your road map monthly. Also, don't hide it in a drawer—make it into a desk blotter or hang it on a door where you can see it daily. Help yourself to be accountable.

Positive Priorities are uplifting choices—they support your body, mind, and spirit and ignite your creative fires. By inviting Positive Priorities into your psychic space, you affirm your self-regard and promote your creative expansion.

> You are not making the change because you are a bad person and you are doing it wrong. You make changes because you love yourself and you want to improve the quality of your life.
> —LOUISE HAY, HEALER AND WRITER

> Synchronicty holds the promise that if we will change within, the patterns in our outer life will change also.
> —JEAN SHINODA BOLEN, AUTHOR

Subtracting Serenity Stealers

To clear your creative channel, you must get rid of the things in your life that don't work and that compromise your creative power.

Keys

- Watching for Signs of Burnout
- Assessing Your Relationship to the Creative Process
- Coping with Unavoidable Serenity Stealers
- Examining Why You Can't Let Go of a Negative Choice

*The first step in starting an enterprise is to clear the space
for it, or till the ground. This clearing process is a must....
We like to think just forging ahead is going to be enough
to start, but when you run into gnarled old roots where
your new plants need to grow, you've got problems.*

—BARRIE DOLNICK, *SIMPLE SPELLS FOR SUCCESS*

*N*egative life choices steal your peace of mind and eclipse your well-being. So in this chapter, you are going to learn about the Power of Subtraction. Here I encourage you to get rid of everything you neither need nor want in your life. This includes anything from old sneakers to outmoded dreams. To create a life of positive choices, you must let go of whatever blocks your creative zest.

First a lesson in stress management. Stress is your body's physical reaction to the demands and pressures of the day. These demands and pressures are called "stressors," and they differ for each of us. Stress happens when your body reacts to stressors as if it were being physically threatened; it prepares for action. This stress reaction comes from your perception that something is threatening your physical or emotional safety. You may react with intense stress symptoms appropriate for a situation like being attacked by a tiger, when in reality you just erased the design program on your computer—frustrating but not fatal.

Challenge: BODY SIGNALS

Write a description of what happens to your body when
you're confronted by a demand or pressure, like too much to
do or fear of failure. If you prefer, you can draw a picture of
your distress, using colors and lots of detail. Try to identify
the ways that your body signals to you that you are over-
stressed and need to tune into what's happening for you.

What you just depicted is your individual stress response, a fin-
gerprint of your physical stress pattern. When your body starts

sending you these signals, it's time to take action. It may be hard to believe, but you have both negative and positive stress reactions. Negative stress responses include feeling anxious or scared. But adrenaline also flows with positive stressors, such as starting a business, falling in love with an idea, or painting a gorgeous sunset for the first time.

Watching for Signs of Burnout

Too much of either positive or negative stress can result in stress overload, commonly known as "burnout." Burnout occurs when you blow your circuits and feel physically and emotionally exhausted. If you say things like, "I used to love my work and now I can't see the point" or "I can't get out of bed anymore," you may be burned out. Work or career burnout happens when you begin to question the meaning and value of your work. If you strive endlessly to meet unrealistic expectations, you may come to a standstill. As uncomfortable as it is, burnout can often launch dramatic positive changes. When your body and psyche sound the alarm, your job is to listen and redirect your life.

Challenge: BURNOUT WARNING SIGNS

Simply circle any of these warning signals you regularly experience in your life and add up the total.

1. Difficulty getting up in the morning
2. Frequently being late for a job or for beginning your creative work
3. Skipping your job or creative work time
4. Irritability or quickness to anger
5. Forgetfulness
6. Frequent illnesses or aches and pains
7. Inflexibility or resistance to change
8. Boredom
9. Frustration

10. Fatigue

11. Feeling unappreciated

12. Hopelessness and detachment

13. Tension

14. Being accident-prone

15. Procrastination

16. Increased alcohol or drug consumption

All of us have difficulty getting up certain mornings, when it's raining out or we have a dreaded meeting ahead of us, but pay attention if there's a pattern. If you have a total of three or more warning signals that you experience on a regular basis, then it's time to start problem solving. Stay tuned.

Burnout impairs access to your inventive creative self. Burnout fogs creative clarity and needs to be resolved to free your potential. The kinds of people who are especially vulnerable to burnout are people who are conscientious with high or unrealistic expectations for themselves. People who are irresponsible usually don't get overly stressed because they're not that invested in the first place.

Many creative women are at high risk for burnout. There are three major behavior patterns that may signal your vulnerability. The first pattern is superachieving.

If you are a superachiever, you work as hard as you can until your work is done, even if it risks your health and well-being. High-pressure responsibilities or agreeing to unrealistic deadlines for creative projects are common predicaments for superachievers. Instead of renegotiating or setting realistic limits, the superachiever works beyond the point of exhaustion in order to meet the expectations.

A second formula for burnout is overscheduling your life. A classic example is the superwoman with the sixty-hour-a-week job, a husband, two kids, a dog, a goldfish, elderly parents, a Girl Scout troop, church committees, and a passion for metal sculpting. Who comes last? She does, with sculpting as a close second. The gateway out of this madness is learning to say "No."

> You take your life into your own hands, and what happens? A terrible thing: no one to blame.
> —ERICA JONG, WRITER

186

The final pattern evolves from the philosophy "No one else can do it as well as I can." If you live by this axiom then you probably can't delegate, can't negotiate for help, have perfectionist standards, and may try to manage everything all alone. Who wouldn't collapse under all that stress? Many creative women are entrepreneurs doing all of their own creative work as well as their own marketing, billing, and taxes. Making sound choices about what can be delegated and choosing the right people helps us to let go and experience the luxury of support. By not training others appropriately or selecting the wrong team of people to work with you, you may create the self-fulfilling prophecy that no one else *can* do it but you. Try sharing your load with a competent assistant or partner who has both the ability and the willingness to do the job, and notice the difference.

If you are an overscheduling superachiever with a "No one can help me" motto, watch out. You may already be burned out or on your way. For most people, creativity and innovation thrive in serenity and calm, although some people enjoy the energy of deadlines. Since creative work is fresh and risky and may go through a series of rejections, you need your life to be in good order so you can handle the roller coaster ride. Again, you have to confront the caretaker versus creator dilemma and make yourself and the choices in your life top priority. Managing your stress demands that you take exquisite care of yourself and your creative powers. Awareness of how you interact with both positive and negative stressors illuminates what kind of self-protection you need. Charting your unique style and vulnerabilities helps you become head navigator of your own life.

Transformational leader Shakti Gawain talked quite openly about her burnout: "Burnout has definitely been a big issue. Having too much responsibility, working too hard, and being exhausted kills my creativity. I need to separate more from those workaholic parts of myself—the teacher, the giver, the world savior—and stay more in touch with the other parts of myself that want time to relax, to play, be quiet, and enjoy solitude and intimacy. The more I am recognizing and allowing those parts to come forth, the more I stay in balance."

Overworking has also challenged Maureen Murdock, who got sick trying to juggle workshops, writing, a psychotherapy practice, and teaching, all high-intensity. Like Shakti, Maureen wants to create more space for her inner life: "I'm originally a New Yorker, and the biggest challenge for me is to deal with my driver and to try to temper my muse. The muse doesn't take into consideration that we're human and in physical form. When I get a bee in my bonnet to do a project, that's what I do. I just turned fifty last year and I hope in this decade I can really learn more about balance."

Challenge: LIFE CHANGE REVIEW

Another catalyst for burnout is too much change in too short a time span. You need to be aware of the impact of change on your creative process. Adapting to multiple changes may drain your energy, even if it's wonderful change, since you are using lots of coping skills to make the transition. Think about how many changes you have experienced this past year.

Circle any of these changes, either positive or negative, that you have had to handle the past twelve months.

1. Death of a spouse or close family member
2. Purchasing real estate or a new business
3. Personal injury or illness
4. Marriage or commitment to a relationship
5. Recognition of personal achievement including awards, promotions, or goal attainment
6. Change in the health of a family member
7. Pregnancy or parenthood including adoption, stepchildren, or caring for another family member
8. Change in financial status, either an increase or decrease in net worth
9. Career or job change or shift in work focus or aspirations
10. Divorce or the end of a significant relationship

11. Job loss or the failure or rejection of a creative project

12. Beginning or ending an educational or training program

13. Moving

14. Changing a personal habit: quitting smoking, dieting

15. Legal troubles

Review your results. For some people, achieving a goal is a positive event, while for others it raises terror about vulnerability and becomes a negative stressor. Decide how each of these life changes is positive or negative in their impact on you. Then look at your total score. If you had three or more of these events in your life this past year, a lot of your energy has been preoccupied coping with change. If that's the case, try to put on the brakes and resist tackling any more changes until you feel centered again. You need time to reflect and integrate the new.

Assessing Your Relationship to the Creative Process

Are you one of those creative souls with piles of unfinished creative projects? Then it's time to choose your path and either let go of the old and begin again, or commit to the completion of what's on your desk at the present. Many creative women just ooze with multiple ideas, so managing these ideas becomes an important strategy to develop. You could work on several projects at a time or commit to one project and a timeline.

Pay attention to which project stirs the most passion in you; that may be the one to start with. Many women fear that if they choose one project, they are abandoning the other. In reality, you are just choosing to focus your attention in one place and experience its fullness. So often, working through one project helps us see the next one more clearly. If you are already burned out, resolving the overload in your current life will free up energy for you to then start anew.

Another source of negative stressors may be your relationship with your own creative process. For example, some people work best alone; others need to have people in their vicinity. Some

Courage is the power to let go of the familiar.
—MARY BYRANT, NATIVE AMERICAN LEADER

people work best in big blocks of time, while others like the pressure of short sprints. Artist and writer Ginny O'Brien is clear on how her creative process works: "I can't force creativity—I have to trust my intuition and my unconscious. When I'm working on a project, ideas come to me while I'm gazing out my kitchen window or sitting in silence reflecting. Inspiration may come in the middle of the night. But nothing comes when I'm stressed out or worried that I need to produce. I need to be relaxed." Working with, not against, your creative style is pivotal to success.

Challenge: UNDERSTANDING YOUR CREATIVE STYLE

Circle any items that are problems for you in your creative work.

1. I have no clear creative goals.
2. My work space is disorganized, uncomfortable, or not conducive to my creative process.
3. My creative work comes last in my life.
4. I have too much to do and too little time to do it.
5. I don't know what to do next.
6. The fear of failure haunts me.
7. My creative flow is blocked.
8. I'm not challenged or excited by the work I'm doing.
9. I have to do everything myself.
10. It seems I move from one deadline to the next.
11. I fear the rejection or criticism of my work.
12. I'm not getting paid enough for my work.
13. My work is so easy that I don't deserve to get paid for it.
14. I don't have the skills I need to do my creative work and/or manage the business end.
15. I spend too much time on paperwork, administration, teaching, client services, traveling, or other responsibilities, and don't have enough time to create.

> Act boldly and unseen forces will come to your aid.
> —DOROTHEA BRANDE, WRITER

16. I feel like I've lost control over my creative process.

17. I feel pressure from others about spending too much time on my creative work.

18. I'm not meeting my personal creative goals.

19. I'm tired of having to constantly market my creative work.

20. I work all the time, and my life is out of balance.

Note whether these stressors are internal or external. The fear of rejection is an internal stressor, while pressure from others is an external stressor. Getting as clear as possible about how you work protects your precious creative impulses from being eclipsed by too much negative stress.

Now it's time to recognize your personal Serenity Stealers—people, tasks, situations, or environments that drain your creative potential. All forward growth begins with letting go.

Letting go of all the things in your life that don't support your creativity is a powerful stance. You evolve every day into a new being and many of the people, projects, and beliefs in your life no longer reflect your present self. Deep down, you know what disturbs your inner peace and what you need to cast off. Serenity Stealers siphon off your life force into destructive tributaries and undermine the potency of your creative stirrings.

Step 1 is to identify your personal Serenity Stealers and then strategize ways to avoid them. For example, some of the women I interviewed love cooking and find it soothing and expansive. Others don't even do it; they eat out. Harpist Deborah Henson-Conant even has a Museum of Burnt Food on her Web site, signifying her abandonment of cooking. We have much more power to manage our lives when we give ourselves permission to subtract things we don't enjoy.

Challenge: YOUR MAGIC WAND

To help you to acknowledge your personal list of Serenity Stealers, imagine that you have a magic wand and you can banish ten things in your life without negative consequences. What

> We need to find the courage to say "NO" to the things and people that are not serving us if we want to rediscover ourselves and live our lives with authenticity.
> —BARBARA DE ANGELIS, WRITER

people, places, beliefs, challenges, or experiences would you like to get rid of? Walk around your home or office practicing making things disappear—the garden that's overgrown, the junk in your closet, the bill-paying routine that doesn't work, or the messages on your answering machine from people that you really don't want to call back. Wave your imaginary wand at the incompetent secretary whom you don't have the courage to fire, or the filing projects you dread tackling. Imagine how you would feel if all of these negative stressors were out of your life! Be candid. It's your interaction with these challenges that creates the dilemmas. Simply write your list in your notebook; write down anything that comes to mind, even if it seems like nonsense. Keep going until you find your top ten Serenity Stealers. If you feel stuck, write about feeling stuck; it will lead you closer to the truth. Don't critique your fantasies, just write them down. This is simply a starting point, not a commitment to action (yet).

Now, with this list of ten Serenity Stealers, note down next to each one what that Serenity Stealer "costs" you. For example, it could be inner peace, self-respect, time, energy, or money. Serenity Stealers operate as negative life choices, even if you didn't originally select them. By not eliminating these negative choices, how is your creativity losing out?

Rank these Serenity Stealers from one through ten, with one being the most personally upsetting Serenity Stealer of all. Then identify the one that feels the hardest to eliminate as well as the one that feels the easiest to get rid of. Imagine your life without these negative choices and then focus on invoking the Power of Subtraction.

One of my clients, Betsy, complained that she couldn't find enough time to paint her lovely watercolor birdhouses—a common cry among women juggling multiple roles. While Betsy currently made her birdhouses as gifts for friends and family, her dream was to eventually run a profitable business selling them. One of Betsy's Serenity Stealers was her garden club committee, run by an out-spoken, intimidating neighbor. Betsy hated this committee because the chairwoman was a master delegator-dumper, and Betsy always came home with lists of phone calls and errands to cram into her already busy days. This committee drudgery stole time away from her beloved birdhouses. As usual, the situation was complicated. This committee was beautifying the park where Betsy's children played, and she believed in the value of the project.

When I pinned Betsy down with my best coaching question, "What do you really want?" she admitted that she wanted to free herself from the tyranny of this woman. I asked her how many hours a week this committee was tying up, and Betsy calculated that it was almost four hours a week, essentially half a day. I asked Betsy if she felt like she had made enough of a contribution to the park project and she squirmed on that point.

Then a brainstorm hit me and I said, "What about making a birdhouse for the children to enjoy in the park and have that be your final contribution to the park? Plus, it will be great promotion for your budding business." Betsy smiled, and agreed to donate the birdhouse of her choice, install it herself, and subtract the committee from her life.

Often creative solutions emerge once you have the courage to tell the truth about what distresses you. You always have the right to avoid or alleviate your Serenity Stealers, simply because you choose to.

Resigning from a committee may seem like a low-stakes item. Often though, eliminating low-stakes Serenity Stealers can be great practice for tackling the giant ones. Think about how empowering Betsy's decision was for her. She claimed four hours a week for her creative work *and* had the opportunity to create a special birdhouse for a cause she believes in. Both actions pulled her life forward in a growth-inducing direction. Most of the women I interviewed had

If you play it safe in life, you've decided that you don't want to grow anymore.
—SHIRLEY HUFSTEDLER, LAWYER

That's the risk you take if you change: that people you've been involved with won't like the new you. But other people who do will come along.
—LISA ALTHER, NOVELIST

already cleared out a lot of their Serenity Stealers in pursuit of their creative commitments. They had gotten rid of unsupportive husbands or lovers, non-nourishing outside activities, and guilt about not doing housework. This, I believe, is one of the reasons they have achieved the levels of success they have.

In addition to resigning from boards, ceramist and devoted wife, mother, and grandmother June Levinson has gotten rid of stuff that she no longer needs or wants so she can focus on her family and her pots. "I continually try to get rid of excessive things from the past. I'm also trying not to be with people who are negative about what I'm doing, especially old friends who have no interest in the creative part of me. They're actually irritated with it because it takes you from them. Art is a very jealous mistress. But the fact is that if you're into your art, and that's what you want to do, you need people in your life who support that passion."

Lucia Capacchione lives in quaint Cambria, California, because it calms her spirit and fuels her work. Yet she also promotes her books by traveling and must manage her travel very carefully to alleviate the stress of a workshop tour. "My energy is drained by environments that are too packed with people and all of the crazy energy that's in a city. I'm learning to manage it pretty well right now, just by timing things and getting to cities a day in advance and resting before I do any speaking. I also reserve days for playing and enjoying the city I'm in, going to museums, parks, special places, and shopping. But my primary goal is to teach in retreat centers," says Lucia. She also gets invited to cities she has no interest in visiting and therefore declines those invitations. Self-protection is a key value for her and has allowed her to create so prolifically.

Serenity Stealers come in all kinds of forms, including negative beliefs. Negative beliefs can haunt you and paralyze your creative expression. Beliefs like the notion that you have to have a secure full-time job in order to survive financially or that no one will appreciate your work destroy the trust between you and your inner knowing. Women who succeed on the creative path find ways to defy the negative beliefs that raise their anxiety levels, eclipse their confidence, or keep their work stale. They refuse to submit to the demon voice that may say their work is garbage, and they have also wrestled with monetary and artistic challenges.

Remember that action diminishes fear; sometimes you need to confront a belief emanating from a family or societal myth and blast your way through it, step by step.

A common axiom that diverts too many women from creative careers is the fear of the "starving artist syndrome." Clearly, many creative careers present unique challenges in self-employment as well as tremendous perseverance, but if that is your calling, you'll find a way. As Barbara Sher says, "Lasting is the essential factor in success."

Challenge: SUBTRACTING BELIEFS

If you have a belief that you'd like to subtract from your life, start by writing a history of it. Who gave it to you in the first place? Whom do you know who lives by that belief and whom do you know who defies it? How does this belief fit with your creative urges? How does it suppress your personal power and initiative? What's positive about it? How might it be preventing you from taking risks in your creative life?

Don't let limiting beliefs stand in your way. Cheryl loved flowers. Her house was filled with them, both silk and real, and she dressed in them, decorated in them, and frequented flower shops year-round. When she came to see me for coaching, she was working unhappily as a nurse manager. We finally got to the flowers. I asked her what would give her the most pleasure to do with her love of flowers and she replied that she'd like to handpaint furniture, but she could never make money doing it. Since I love hand-painted floral furniture, I knew it was very pricey, and I challenged her limited thinking. I sent her out to research artists doing work she admired and she returned excited by the prospects and stunned by the prices she saw. Like any business, success depends on numerous factors; you need a location or trade show tour and a skill level to make it, but it can be done. Step 1 for her involved

> Trouble is the common denominator of living. It is the great equalizer.
> —ANN LANDERS, COLUMNIST

taking lessons, learning about the materials, and developing some prototypes. She started by selling small items in the hospital gift store; now she has her own studio and is slowly expanding. Once she changed her belief and plugged into a plan, her reality changed.

Coping with Unavoidable Serenity Stealers

What about those Serenity Stealers that you can't avoid or alleviate, like caring for a demanding elderly mother? Again, analyze what this situation "costs" you: time for yourself, aggravation from your mother's constant complaints, or simply not enjoying your time together. Is there a way to fix or alleviate any of these problems? Are you taking on too much of the responsibility yourself? Women are often the family caretakers of their elderly parents. Do you need to call up your brothers and insist that they help too? Do you need to move your mother closer to you to make contact easier? Are there medications that can help your mother with depression? Do you need to set up a schedule and stick to it or hire a support team for her? Can you think of new ways to spend time with your mother that would be mutually rewarding and less stressful? Have a family meeting and construct a plan that shares the responsibilities and prevents you from burning out and resenting your mother. Wrestling with your Serenity Stealers often invites creative solutions. Don't stay passive—try some experiments and banish the martyr in you.

There are also the enormous disasters that shake you to the very core. Designer Diane Ericson's life has been rocked with life-changing events for the past decade, which is why she says, "I get that all we can control is what we do with what happens. And that's been an incredibly important, painful, joyful, intense lesson for me." Her journey began ten years ago, when her then-husband announced that he didn't want to be married and left her with two small children and the agony of having to give up the house of her dreams. Three years after surviving those losses, she met her soul mate at an airport. Diane describes that relationship: "My soul mate was someone I felt like I'd known for thirty years. I had never been with anyone who could be with who I was, and he could. We met in an airport in Salt Lake City and within ten minutes he looked at me and said, 'Where have you been?' Within six months we were recreating a family—and then he died quite suddenly." A month later her ex-husband decided he wanted the kids, and she finally decided that it was best for everyone if they spent some time with him.

A few years later, after welcoming her kids back home, her home was leveled by a flood, and they were left homeless. Diane says, "I just felt like the universe had said, 'You know what, we need her to be a little different than she is now. Don't worry about the subtle stuff, just blast her. Don't torture her with just a little bit here and there.' I lost 85 percent of my belongings and my car overnight." Nevertheless, Diane emanates a joy and fascination with life and learning that is contagious. She has moved on from these devastations to create a life of work she loves, a family of mutual nurturing, and a web of support for herself that empowers her endless creative flow.

Particularly challenging Serenity Stealers require that you acknowledge their wear and tear on your body and psyche, so be sure to pamper yourself. Janet Hagberg takes one-half day each week to pray, write in her journal, be totally quiet and listen for guidance from her intuition. Take a walk, rent a great video, visit your friends, sneak in a nap, or cut back your work schedule temporarily—whatever it takes to take great care of you. Monitor the impact of the old caretaker versus creativity scripts that most of us grew up with and invent a new paradigm that works for you and models healthy behavior for your daughters and other young women. Even difficult challenges may contain a hidden gift—if you look for it. For example, many adults who care for their elderly parents reap a new closeness with them and it may provide grist for your creative mill later.

> To gain that which is worth having, it may be necessary to lose everything else.
> —BERNADETTE DEVLIN, WRITER

Examining Why You Can't Let Go of a Negative Choice

If you find it impossible to let go of a Serenity Stealer that you do have a choice about, you need to look for insight into the possible silent payoff. Sometimes a negative choice serves a purpose. You have to discover its underlying meaning before you can move on. For example, if you can never find time to write that novel or try a new marketing idea, you may be shielding yourself from feeling incompetent. You may stay in an intolerable job because you don't want to face the reality that you need to change careers. To admit the underlying payoff for hanging onto negative choices, you must be totally honest with yourself. Several techniques can help you to gain insight.

Write a pro and con list for your choice as if you hadn't yet decided whether or not to add this choice to your life.

Crystal, a client, discovered that the only good things about her despicable job were her measly paycheck and the geranium plant on her desk that was a birthday gift from her staff. But when she dug deeper, she realized that her job gave her prestige, which she valued. So she had to decide if she wanted to continue sacrificing her happiness on a daily basis just to impress other people. She longed to pursue her interest in filmmaking, but it would mean casting off her managerial identity and possibly starting at the bottom to get experience.

Soul-wrenching jobs crush your creative spirit and prevent you from engaging with work that stimulates your natural talents. The world needs your perceptions and passion. Analyzing your attachment to your negative choices frees you to tackle the right decision.

If you're still unclear, try another tactic. *Write two pages about why you must have this negative choice in your life. What are its benefits, conscious and unconscious? Write down anything that comes to mind, however weird. Then go back and circle the key concepts and look for patterns.*

For my client Paula, her Serenity Stealer was her choice to work at home. As a working mother, she wanted to be available to her son in case of an emergency and hired an at-home baby-sitter while she worked in another room. She owned a landscape architecture business, but because she is an extrovert, she lost steam on her own by 10 A.M. Too often she would start housecleaning instead of marketing or send her son's baby-sitter home early. Every day evoked an internal war in her mind. Once she confronted the failure of her plan, she feared that she couldn't afford an office. Of course, with her present set-up, she wasn't earning any money anyway. She kept trying to make herself fit the work-at-home paradigm, and the reality didn't compute. What she really wanted was to be part of a team. After some questing, she joined an architecture firm with a suite of offices in an appealing building. Her new office was close to home, which was one of her criteria for comfort, and she worked a half-day on Saturday (to better serve her clients), which allowed her to spend an afternoon of quality time with her son during the week. An unforeseen benefit was that her husband and son discovered a mutual love of science and began to spend hours at the museum on Saturdays. Last, she converted her home office into an exercise room. Once she set herself free from a rigid model of how things "should" be for her, she was able to transform the actuality so it worked for everyone.

If you still feel baffled or unsure of how to proceed, try this strategy. *To help you make those difficult decisions about the items on your subtraction list, keep a detailed Serenity Stealer diary for two weeks. Note down the following about each episode with your Serenity Stealer: Day, Time, Location, Your Physical Reaction, Your Emotional Reaction, How You Cope, The "Real" Problem, and Resolution. See if you can find the true problem behind your Serenity Stealer.*

Kara, a client, feared she could never become an effective speaker and fulfill her dream of a selling cookware as her own business. When she kept a diary for two weeks about how inexpressive and timid she was in meetings, in personal relationships, and with her horrid boss, she saw that her fear of voicing her opinions was ruining her life. Every single day, Kara felt ashamed and guilty for not mastering this fear. After keeping this diary for two weeks, she appeared in my office wearing a nametag that said "Doormat," ready to learn assertiveness and presentation skills. She now has a successful business.

Knowledge is power in the battle with Serenity Stealers. Careful study should coax the hard-core facts and their meaning to the surface. You might want to share your diary with a trusted friend or counselor to get another point of view. So often, we are too close to our own mind games to see the big picture. Awareness begins the process of change. In two weeks, you certainly will be further ahead.

Once you have eliminated all of the Serenity Stealers you can most easily subtract, tackle the most challenging ones. My client, Gwen, felt trapped in a marriage with a man who criticized her every move. She wanted to save marine life and he thought her interest in the environment was futile because all species were already doomed. Gwen feared that she wouldn't be able to take care of herself without him, yet knew in her soul that her relationship with her husband was toxic. By keeping a Serenity Stealer diary, Gwen realized that she depended on him for cooking and financial management and feared she could never accomplish these tasks on her own, let alone go back to school to study marine biology. She agreed to try an experiment with three strategies to help her minimize the power of her fear: she signed up for an adult education series at her local aquarium, asked her friends to each teach her one dinner recipe, and met with a financial planner three times for an overview of Finance 101. She is still conflicted about whether or not to divorce her husband, but these three initiatives put her on stronger footing from which to choose. Remember, difficult choices and transitions are part of life—no one promised any of us that it would be easy.

To help you proactively manage your Serenity Stealer, explore these five questions:

1. How have you already tried to manage this stressor and why did these tactics fail?

By non-judgmentally acknowledging your faltered efforts, you get a better sense of how to approach an obstacle. Let's say you rented a pottery studio with the goal of making flower pots three times a week, but you never went. Take a moment to explore the truth about your choice not to go. Was the studio too far away, too cold, or lacking the right equipment? Did you feel unsupported by the staff, or uninspired by the environment? Gently, keep asking those questions that will help you to get clear about why your previous action plans haven't worked. Don't just decide that you're lazy or inadequate. Every action plan is an experiment. If it doesn't work, figure out why. Solve the problem rather than blaming yourself and giving up. Change is difficult and you can only move at your own pace.

2. What personal barriers to success must you overcome? Circle those that apply for you:

   a. Trying to solve the wrong problem

   b. Procrastination

   c. Not taking responsibility for creating or contributing to this conflict

   d. Giving up too easily

   e. Feeling overwhelmed by the dilemma

   f. Not asking for help when you need it

   g. Not communicating exactly what you want

   h. Having unrealistic expectations of yourself

   i. Not rewarding yourself for progress

See if any of these barriers ring true for you and rectify them. Often, we expect change instantaneously when long-term change is usually gradual and organic.

3. What new skills would help you?

When you initiate change in your life, you often need to learn new skills. Opening up to new ideas and strategies is not a sign of weakness, but rather a courageous pathway to discovering growth. How do you learn best? What kinds of books, visual aids, teachers, or experiences can bolster your ability to master this problem?

4. What kinds of support systems would increase your chances for success?

In addition to new skills, when you navigate change, you need extra support from people. Think about what kinds of support people, groups, or systems would help you to meet your goal. Support systems are a key ingredient in the change process, because they help to keep you motivated and on track. If you are one of those "only I can do this right" people, asking for support can be a breakthrough in your pursuit of well-being. Be sure to identify what kind of help you want as well as what kind you don't want.

5. What decisions can you make today and put into action that will move you closer toward resolution?

These answers comprise a draft of your first action plan. An action plan is never set in stone. It is meant to be flexible and change as you do. Over the course of your life, you will change stressors and action plans. These revisions symbolize the developmental journey that is life.

In the next chapter, you will have the opportunity to finalize and actively begin to implement your goals. Clinging to negative choices or fearing change holds you back and stifles the seedlings in your heart. Getting rid of Serenity Stealers clears the space to explore and experience your Positive Priorities. Addition and subtraction are powerful life-enhancing strategies since they confirm that you are indeed the creator of your days on this Earth.

Planning to Achieve Your Goals

This is the final chapter in the Third Gateway. Now you have all the information you need to implement a plan of action to achieve your creative goals and a life of abundance.

Keys

- Deciding about Sharing Your Creative Work
- Setting Creative Goals
- Committing Your Time
- Tackling Procrastination
- Celebrating Your Creative Power

The paths we take depend on our
own definitions of success.

—Virginia O'Brien, *Success on Our Own Terms*

By now you have learned many of the success strategies of highly creative women. You have a much greater understanding about how to create your own rendezvous with your creative self. Now it's time to take action and commit to goals for yourself. No more excuses! You've heard the stories and you have the insights. Let's give you the tools to make it happen. You may want to pick a partner or set up a mutual coaching group of other creative women and work on these goals together. Even a telephone or e-mail check-in once a week with one other person can keep you accountable and productive.

Challenge: Personal Creativity Creed

The goal of this exercise is to help you to develop a series of personal operating principles for your creative self-expression. By answering the following questions, you can then write a creed for yourself:

1. What is your personal creative mission? What do you hope to accomplish as a creative conduit with your work and your life?

2. What are your beliefs about creativity in general and your creativity specifically? How does your spirituality influence your creativity?

3. What are your creative strengths? What are your creative stumbling blocks?

4. What are the three most important lessons you have learned in this book?

5. What part of the creative cycle are you in currently?

Summarize all of your thoughts and write a paragraph that captures your creative purpose and highlights your gifts and your challenges as a creative woman. Complete this sentence: My Creativity Creed is . . .

Deciding about Sharing Your Creative Work

Before you commit to specific goals for yourself, I encourage you to think carefully about if and how you want to share your creative work. Are you doing your creative work for pleasure, profit, or both? Do you want to market your work and if so, how? While market research is an essential component to a well-designed marketing plan, I encourage people to think carefully about their own style first. Many an entrepreneur has failed by trying to follow someone else's formula, one that didn't fit her personality.

Juanita, a client of mine, is a true introvert, so she prefers talking to people about her graphics business one on one, rather than trying to shine at a large gathering. Think about the following questions to help you to determine your priorities.

> You have to erect a fence and say, "Okay, scale this."
> —LINDA RONSTADT, SINGER

Challenge: YOUR SHARING GOALS

1. Who and where is the audience you want to reach with your work?

2. What is the message in your work?

3. What business are you in, e.g., entertainment, education, enlightenment, fine arts, medicine, business services, or a combination?

4. What percentage of time do you want to spend creating versus something else, like marketing? Create your own time formula and write your own job description from it. Be sure to include time for yourself and vacations. What tasks need to be delegated or how many employees/contractors do you need to make your business work?

5. How much money do you want to make in the future? Remember, you need to project your gross income minus your business expenses and allot sufficient funds for taxes.

6. All of us could market ourselves around the clock. Marketing is an endless task. How much time and energy are you willing to invest in this process? Write a list of marketing goals as the start of a marketing plan.

7. Do you like public speaking or appearing on television and radio? Are you skilled at presenting yourself or do you need some training? Do you enjoy the limelight or dread it? Perhaps you'd rather write articles than be on the speaking circuit.

8. How do you feel about being away from home? Is travel exciting to you or a chore? What happens to your creative energy when you travel? Many creative women limit their travel to a certain percentage of their time and choose where to go.

9. How is your work best presented? Think innovatively about different models. Do you need a multimedia presentation, a Web site, a workbook, a film, or a sales force?

10. How are you most comfortable presenting your work? What kinds of communications with potential clients or customers feel positive and mutually rewarding to you? Will these preferences work for you in the marketplace? Try some experiments. As more of the marketplace is influenced by the Internet, some exciting new possibilities emerge.

Sharing your work offers the potential for another dimension of your creativity. Start by being totally candid with yourself about who you are, and decide how you best form relationships with your clients or customers. I hope that the previous questions illuminated your personal style and preferences. Now you can develop marketing ideas as unique as your work, or you may realize that you simply want to do creative work for yourself or to share with family and friends. Design a plan that keeps you grounded and centered to help you deflect rejection and meet your goals.

Martha, a sculptor, chose a plan of showing her work five times a year in her own home. As her reputation grew and she became more skilled at event planning, these five shows drew more buyers and admirers. Martha loved sharing both her home and her work with her guests as well as being totally in charge of the environment in which she could exhibit her sculptures. She also enjoyed the casual nature of her events and having the opportunity to discuss her work with her guests in a relaxed manner. She did not want to exhibit nationally because she savored the cottage industry feel of her shows.

Could she make more money if she exhibited more widely? Probably, but Martha claims that the tradeoffs of travel and the lack of intimacy with her patrons aren't worth it for her. Try to be as precise as possible about what benefits you want for yourself from your creative process.

> Fill your thoughts with what you want to create, and you will have it.
> —SANAYA ROMAN, WRITER

Setting Creative Goals

Your next step is goal setting. Don't stop reading; this will be a simple guide! Remember goal setting is a process of evolution, and you're in charge of it. We know that the very act of setting goals signals the universe that you're serious, helping you to stay focused and true to your vision.

What is a goal? A goal is simply a statement of intention—a result toward which effort is directed. During her struggle to decide whether or not to stay married to her first husband, Marilyn Veltrop climbed alone to the top of a mountain in Maine where she had a life-changing experience. At the top of that mountain she vowed, "I am going to have a life with more of this ecstasy—this truly expansive connection, energy, and oneness." Marilyn did get a divorce and has met her compelling mission with a new husband, the home of her dreams, and work she loves.

There are seven elements to successful goal setting. Goals must be:

1. *Specific:* State the exact result you want: I will try out for acting roles in three plays this fall.

> Goals are dreams with deadlines.
> —DIANA SCHARF HUNT, WRITER

2. *Measurable:* A behavior or a product that can observed and quantified by amounts or numbers of actions: I will begin an idea book today and write in it twice a week for six months.

3. *Realistic:* Achievable within your time frame and ability: I will spend one month next summer writing a screenplay.

4. *Written Down:* Written in clear, concise language and ideally visible and reviewed daily: (Posted on the refrigerator): I will complete a new portfolio of my photographs by April 1.

5. *Time-limited:* Use exact dates and times for the completion of each action step: I will make twenty-five marketing phone calls to people on my prospect list by 5 P.M. on August 3.

6. *Positive:* Stated in positive rather than negative terms: I will reward myself for composing my song (rather than I will punish myself every time I don't sit at the piano).

7. *Action-oriented:* Broken down into action steps, which are things that need to be done in order to meet the goal: I want to go back to school, and I need to do the following action steps: See a career counselor for an assessment, call and get catalogs, visit schools, check out financial aid options.

Take some time to review all of your answers from all of the *Challenges* in this book or just dive in at this point and write down your top three goals for this year. Then test them out against the seven guidelines listed. Go back to your road map from chapter 10, and write in and highlight these top three goals. Are there any Serenity Stealers that need to be eliminated first? Rework your goals as needed. Of those three goals, break them down into monthly increments with monthly tasks for the span of one year. Don't try to work on more than three at a time. Too many goals are almost worse than none. Trust your intuition, and if three seem like too many, start with one.

Committing Your Time

The trick to managing your time in order to meet your goals involves thinking differently about your daily plan. Each day, you need to separate your activities into goal-directed ones and non–goal-directed ones. Most people let the day overwhelm them and then end up with no time left to work on their goals.

Only you can change this dynamic—no one else will do it for you. If someone put a gun to your head and said they'd shoot you if you didn't paint for thirty minutes every day, you'd do it! As we've discussed however, for women, making creative time a priority requires you believing that you are entitled to it. It also demands that you let go of perfectionism about your job, your dust, or your relationships with others, and give yourself equal priority. We cannot do everything; so we must choose carefully in order to meet our creative goals. To help you see how you spend your time each day so you can police yourself (in case you are sabotaging your own efforts), I have included a daily planning tool on the next page. Photocopy it thirty times and try it for one month.

When you have a dream, you've got to grab it and never let go.
—CAROL BURNETT,
ACTRESS AND
COMEDIENNE

Plans for Today

Date

Monthly Goals

1.

2.

3.

Visualize Achieving These Goals (check off)

Today's Specific Actions Toward Each Goal, including what time you are going to do each one and the desired result:

1.

2.

3.

4.

List Other Time Commitments for the Day (work, appointments, family time, chores, errands, etc.)

Starting time   Ending time   Commitment   Priority, Agreement, Possible

Delegation, or Skip (select one)

New Insights and Goals

Transfer Actions to Next Day

Procrastinations

Note the status of all of your commitments and rank them. Are they a priority or could someone else do it for you? Did you promise to do something for someone? If so, then it's an agreement. Watch what you agree to do in your life and see if you need to make any changes to free up more time. Can you just skip something today or maybe even for a year? Also, transfer what didn't get done today to the next day or to a day when you can actually accomplish the goal. This sheet is great for outsmarting those saboteurs! Watch how you organize your days and notice how much time you make to do your creative work. If you use this daily planning tool faithfully for one month, you will have increased self-awareness of your relationship with time and how to make your creativity a priority in your busy life.

Tackling Procrastination

You should notice any new ideas or insights that pop up for you, as well as a tendency to procrastinate. If you are good at procrastinating, fill out the Procrastination Worksheet that follows.

Procrastination is often indecision. Sometimes we need more information, more support, or a structure to insure we can pursue our goal. Sometimes, though, we have an incorrect goal or we're trying to solve the wrong problem. A woman in one of my Creative Circle groups kept postponing making her blueberry wreaths. After exploring her dilemma, it became apparent that she was bored with them and wanted to experiment with another creative medium. We had to help her work through what she really wanted so she could let go and direct her energy toward a new inspiration. If you find you are procrastinating with your creative work, try the worksheet on the following page to help you zero in on the truth.

I'm tough, ambitious, and know exactly what I want.
—MADONNA, SINGER AND ACTRESS

Procrastination Worksheet

Use one sheet per goal or task

Goal or Task Being Avoided:

Is this goal/task important to you? Why?

What is blocking its completion? Are you ambivalent? Are you afraid? Are you lacking information?
Do you need support or help? Is your saboteur involved?

Solutions

Decision: Select one.

_____ I have decided to complete this goal or task by _____.*

_____ I have decided not to complete this goal/task at this time myself.

     _____ I never plan to do it.

     _____ I am delegating it to someone else.

     _____ I will complete this goal/task in the month of _____.

     _____ I need to gather more information before I can make a decision, and I will complete that

       process in the month of _____.

Swiss Cheese List: Breaking the Task into Manageable Bites

If you've agreed to complete this goal/task, break it down into tiny components and target a completion date for each
one. Be specific and complete.

Component	Due Date	Success/Difficulties:
1.		
2.		
3.		
4.		
5.		

I also recommend that you write down in your notebook a master list of ongoing long-term goals, including your life enhancers. Review them quarterly and on New Year's Day.

Update your road map every month, and keep a current list of Serenity Stealers on hand, since they will change as your life unfolds. A mere ten minutes a day spent tracking your creative time and enriching your life with Positive Priorities will pay off a thousandfold in accomplishments and a stronger sense of your creative self.

Celebrating Your Creative Power

You have now completed the Third Gateway and have the tools to become a highly creative woman. Remember, you are solely responsible for the choices in your life, including if, how, and when you express your creative voice. Don't be afraid to claim your dreams and experiment with your own creative style. Have fun with your creative ideas and make your unfolding a true-life adventure. You are entitled to explore your inspirations and grant them the energy they need. As Dr. Clarissa Pinkola Estés advises, "For those who *must* follow the *via creativa,* the creative path, I say: Go. Go right now, and as soon, and as often as you can. Keep going."

Gather support from others as you take risks and share your process. Slay those Serenity Stealers and saboteurs in your way and charge ahead, knowing that you are part of a community of other creative women wishing you success and abundance! Their passion and mine are infused in this book, cheering you on to experience peak moments with your creative self. You are an original woman. Empower yourself, lean on us, and prosper! As Cathleen Rountree reminds us, "The true secret of creativity is doing it."

Bon chance!

> Your goal should be out of reach but not out of sight.
>
> —ANITA DEFRANTZ,
> OLYMPIC ROWING
> MEDALIST

> I wasn't lucky. I deserved it!
>
> —MARGARET THATCHER,
> FORMER PRIME MINISTER
> OF ENGLAND

Bibliography

Aburdene, Patricia, and John Naisbitt. *Megatrends for Women.* New York: Villard Books, 1992.

Amabile, Teresa M., Ph.D. *Growing Up Creative: Nurturing a Lifetime of Creativity.* New York: Crown Publishers, 1989.

Awiakta, Marilou. *Selu: Seeking the Corn-Mother's Wisdom.* Golden, Colorado: Fulcrum Publishing, 1993.

Baber, Anne, and Lynne Waymon. *Fifty-Two Ways To Connect, Follow-up and Stay In Touch, When You Don't Have Time to Network.* Dubuque, Iowa: Kendall-Hunt, 1993.

_____. *Great Connections: Small Talk and Networking for Business People.* Manassas, Virginia: Impact Publishers, 1992.

Barron, Anthea, Frank Barron, and Alfonso Montuori. *Creators on Creating: Awakening and Cultivating the Imaginative Mind.* New York: Jeremy P. Tarcher/Putnam, 1997.

Bender, Sue. *Plain and Simple: A Woman's Journey to the Amish.* San Francisco, California: Harper & Row Publishers, 1989.

Bepko, Claudia, and Jo-Ann Krestan. *Singing at the Top of Our Lungs.* New York: Harper Collins, 1993.

Bolker, Joan L., ed. *The Writer's Home Companion: An Anthology of the World's Best Writing Advice, from Keats to Kunitz.* New York: Henry Holt, 1997.

Blum, Ralph. *The Book of Runes: A Handbook for the Use of an Ancient Oracle: The Viking Runes.* New York: St. Martin's Press, 1982.

Bowler Hellund, Gail. *Artists' and Writers' Colonies: Retreats, Residencies, and Respites for the Creative Mind.* Hillsboro, Oregon: Blue Heron Publishing, Inc., 1995.

Breathnach, Sarah Ban. *Simple Abundance: A Daybook of Comfort and Joy.* New York: Warner Books, 1995.

_____. *The Simple Abundance Journal of Gratitude.* New York: Warner Books, Inc., 1996.

Bry, Adelaide. *Visualization: Directing the Movies of Your Mind to Improve Your Health, Expand Your Mind, and Achieve Your Life Goals.* New York: Barnes & Noble Books, 1978.

Cameron, Julia. *The Artist's Way: A Spiritual Path to Higher Creativity: A Course in Discovering and Recovering Your Creative Self.* New York: Putnam Publishing, 1992.

_____. *The Vein of Gold: A Journey to Your Creative Heart.* New York: Tarcher/Putnam Publishing, 1996.

Capacchione, Lucia, Ph.D., A.T.R. *The Creative Journal: The Art of Finding Yourself.* North Hollywood, California: Newcastle Publishing Company, Inc., 1989.

_____. *Recovery of Your Inner Child.* New York: Simon & Schuster/Fireside, 1991.

_____. *The Power of Your Other Hand.* North Hollywood, California, Newcastle Publishing Company, Inc. 1988.

Cappadona-Apostolos, Diane, and Lucinda Ebersole. *Women, Creativity, and the Arts: Critical and Autobiographical Perspectives.* New York: Continuum, 1995.

Cassou, Michelle, and Stewart Cubley. *Life, Paint and Passion: Reclaiming the Magic of Spontaneous Expression.* New York: Putnam, 1996.

Dolnick, Barrie. *Simple Spells for Success: Ancient Practices for Creating Abundance and Prosperity.* New York: Harmony House, 1996.

Driscoll, Dawn-Marie, and Carol R. Goldberg. *Members of the Club: The Coming of Age of Executive Women*. New York: Free Press, 1993.

Duerk, Judith. *I Sit Listening to the Wind: Woman's Encounter Within Herself. (Circle of Stone Series.)* San Diego, California: LuraMedia, 1993.

Ealy, Diane C., Ph.D. *The Woman's Book of Creativity*. Berkeley, California: Celestial Arts, 1999.

Epel, Naomi. *Writers Dreaming*. New York: Carol Southern Books,1993.

Estés, Clarissa Pinkola. *The Creative Fire: Myths and Stories about the Cycles of Creativity*. Colorado: Sounds True, 1991. (audio-tape)

_____. *Women Who Run with the Wolves*. New York: Ballantine, 1992.

Field, Shelly. *100 Best Careers for Writers and Artists: Discover Exciting Job Opportunities That Call for Your Creative Talents*. New York: Macmillan, 1998.

Frenier, Carol, R. *Business and the Feminine Principle: The Untapped Resource*. Boston: Butterworth-Heinemann, 1997.

Friedman, Martha. *Overcoming the Fear of Success: Why and How We Defeat Ourselves and What to Do about It*. New York: Seaview Books, 1980.

Fritz, Robert. *The Path of Least Resistance: Learning to Become the Creative Force in Your Own Life*. New York: Fawcett Columbine, 1984.

Gault, Rosette. *Paper Clay*. London: A. and C. Black; Philadelphia: University of Pennsylvania Press; and Australia: Artisan Craft Press, 1998.

Gawain, Shakti. *Creating True Prosperity*. Novato, California: New World Library, 1997.

_____. *Creative Visualization*. New York: Bantam New Age Books, 1982.

_____. *Living in the Light: A Guide to Personal and Planetary Transformation*. Mill Valley, California: Whatever Publishing, Inc., 1986.

_____. *Return to the Garden: A Journey of Discovery.* San Rafael, California: New World Library, 1989.

Giese, Jo. *A Woman's Path.* New York: Golden Books, 1998.

Godfrey, Joline. *No More Frogs to Kiss: 99 Ways to Give Economic Power to Girls.* New York: HarperBusiness, 1995.
_____. *Our Wildest Dreams: Women Entrepreneurs Making Money, Having Fun, Doing Good: A Whole New Definition of Success and an Entirely New Paradigm of Working Life.* New York: HarperBusiness, 1992.

Hagberg, Janet, O. *Real Power: Stages of Personal Power in Organizations.* Salem, Wisconsin: Sheffield Publishing Company, 1994.
_____. *Wrestling with Your Angels: A Spiritual Journey to Great Writing.* Holbrook, Massachusetts: Adams Publishing, 1995.

Harris, Maria. *Dance of the Spirit: The Seven Steps of Women's Spirituality.* New York: Bantam Books, 1989.

Heller, Nancy G. *Women Artists: An Illustrated History.* New York: Abbeville Press Publishers, 1987.

Jeffers, Susan, Ph.D. *Dare to Connect.* New York: Fawcett Columbine, 1992.
_____. *Feel the Fear and Do It Anyway.* New York: Fawcett Columbine, 1987.

Koller, Alice. *An Unknown Woman: A Journey to Self-Discovery.* New York: Bantam Books, 1981.

Lamott, Anne. *Bird by Bird: Some Instructions on Writing and Life.* New York: Anchor Books, Doubleday, 1994.

Lawrence-Lightfoot, Sara. *I've Known Rivers: Lives of Loss and Liberation.* New York: Penguin Books, 1994.

Lerner Goldhor, Harriet, Ph.D. *The Dance of Anger: A Woman's Guide to Changing the Patterns of Intimate Relationships.* New York: Harper & Row, Publishers, Inc., 1985.

Lloyd, Carol. *Creating a Life Worth Living.* New York: HarperCollins Publishers, Inc., 1997.

Madden, Chris Casson. *A Room of Her Own: Women's Personal Spaces.* New York: Clarkson Potter, 1997.

Maddox, Rebecca. *Ink Your Dreams.* New York: Penguin, 1996.

McMeekin, Gail, M.S.W. *Positive Choices: From Stress to Serenity.* Boston: Guided Growth, 1992. (audiotape)

Michels, Caroll. *How to Survive and Prosper as an Artist: Selling Yourself Without Selling Your Soul.* New York: Henry Holt, 1997.

Morscher, Betsy, and Barbara Schindler-Jones. *Risk-Taking for Women.* New York: Everest House, 1982.

Murdock, Maureen. *The Heroine's Journey: Woman's Quest for Wholeness.* Boston: Shambhala, 1990.

_____. *The Heroine's Journey Workbook.* Boston: Shambhala, 1998.

O'Brien, Virginia. *Success on Our Own Terms: Tales of Extraordinary, Ordinary Business Women.* New York: John Wiley & Sons, Inc., 1998.

Packer, Duane, and Sanaya Roman. *Creating Money: Keys to Abundance.* Tiburon, California: HJ Kramer, Inc., 1988.

Perera Brinton, Sylvia. *Descent to the Goddess: A Way of Initiation for Women.* Toronto, Canada: [AU: Publisher?], 1981.

Phillips, Jan. *Marry Your Muse: Making a Lasting Commitment to Your Creativity.* Wheaton, Illinois: Quest Books, 1997.

Ponder, Catherine. *The Dynamic Laws of Prosperity: Forces That Bring Riches to You.* Englewood Cliffs, New Jersey: Prentice-Hall, Inc., 1962.

_____. *Open Your Mind to Prosperity.* Unity Village, Missouri: Unity Books, 1971.

Rand, Ayn. *The Virtue of Selfishness: A New Concept of Egoism.* New York: New American Library-Signet Book, 1964.

Rosenberg Pierce, Judith. *A Question of Balance: Artists and Writers on Motherhood.* Watsonville, California: Papier-Mâché Press, 1995.

Rountree, Cathleen. *Coming Into Our Fullness: On Women Turning Forty.* Freedom, California: The Crossing Press, 1991.

_____. *On Women Turning 50: Celebrating Mid-Life Discoveries.* New York: Harper San Francisco, 1993.

_____. *On Women Turning 60: Embracing the Age of Fulfillment*. Three Rivers Press, 1998.

Schade Royce, Edith. *May Sarton's Well: Writings of May Sarton*. Watsonville, California: Papier-Mâché Press, 1994.

Shaughnessy, Susan. *Walking on Alligators: A Book on Meditations for Writers*. New York: Harper Collins Publishers, 1993.

Shaw, Alison. *Vineyard Summer*. Boston: Little, Brown and Company, 1994.

Sher, Barbara. *It's Only Too Late If You Don't Start Now: How to Create Your Second Life After Forty*. New York: Delacorte Press, 1998.

Sher, Barbara, and Annie Gottlieb. *Wishcraft: How to Get What You Really Want*. New York: Ballantine Books, 1986.

Sher, Barbara, and Barbara Smith. *I Could Do Anything If I Only Knew What It Was: How to Discover What You Really Want and How to Get It*. New York: Delacorte Press, 1994.

Shore, Lesley Irene, Ph.D. *Healing the Feminine: Reclaiming Woman's Voice*. St. Paul, Minnesota: Llewellyn Publications, 1995.
_____. *Tending Inner Gardens: The Healing Art of Feminist Psychology*. Binghamton, New York: Haworth Press, 1994.

Shulman, Alix Kates. *Drinking the Rain*. New York: Farrar Straus Giroux, 1995.

Sinetar, Marsha. *Elegant Choices, Healing Choices*. Mahwah, New Jersey: Paulist Press, 1988.
_____. *To Build the Life You Want, Create the Work You Love: The Spiritual Dimension of Entrepreneuring*. New York: St. Martin's Press, 1995.

Stone Levi, Sidra, Ph.D. *Ending the Tyranny of the Inner Patriarch*. New York: Penny Price Media, 1995. (video)
_____. *The Shadow King: The Invisible Force That Holds Women Back: Ending the Tyranny of the Inner Patriarch*. Mill Valley, California: Nataraj Publishing, 1997.

Ueland, Brenda. *If You Want to Write: A Book about Art, Independence and Spirit*. St. Paul, Minnesota: Graywolf Press, 1938.

Williamson, Marianne. *A Woman's Worth*. New York: Ballantine Books, 1993.

Wolf, Naomi. *Fire with Fire: The New Female Power and How It Will Change the Tenty-First Century*. New York: Random House, 1993.

Woolf, Virginia. *A Room of One's Own*. 1929. London: The Hogarth Press, 1991.

Yudkin, Marcia. *Marketing Online*. New York: Plume/Penguin, 1995.

_____. *Six Steps to Free Publicity—and Dozens of Other Ways to Win Free Media Attention for You or Your Business*. New York: Plume/Penguin, 1994.

Acknowledgments

To all of the women who volunteered their time, their wisdom, and their stories for this book, in the service of mentoring other women. As a team of cowriters, we have given women many tools for self-expression and fulfillment. This is very much a collaborative project.

To Conari Press, and especially to my insightful editor, Mary Jane Ryan, for having the vision to publish this book that inspires women to claim their creative voices. I am honored to be included in your selection of books that make a difference.

To my husband, Rusty Street, for his steadfast support of my dream to write this book. He cheered me on endlessly, insisted that I take naps, managed the details of our lives, and set important boundaries for me on days when I couldn't. I will be eternally grateful.

To my personal editor, Marcia Yudkin, for her expert guidance, as well as my readers and incredible friends, Deborah Knox and Gail Jones, for their insightful comments and support of this project. To Rachel Travers for her many hours transcribing tapes, and Athena Dimas and Trisha Keogh for essential administrative support.

A special thanks to Carol Frenier, Deborah Knox, and Karen Speerstra for their synchronistic dance that lead me to Conari Press.

To my daily e-mail buddy and friend, Marilyn Veltrop, for her listening and profound wisdom, her organic approach, and her daily reminders about the importance of balance as we each worked on our parallel creative projects.

To my friends and family for understanding my need to be a hermit to complete this book and their encouragement and support along the way, as well as all their referrals to creative women.

To my Sophia group for holding the intention of this book and sharing their own brilliance and spiritual perspectives on creation and divinity.

To my many wonderful women clients and workshop participants over the past twenty-five years, my great appreciation for our mutual learning and connection. All your stories have been disguised.

Index

*G*ail McMeekin, M.S.W., L.I.C.S.W., is a career and creativity coach with more than twenty-five years of experience helping clients discover and achieve their personal, professional, and creative goals. Her specialty is empowering creative women to fulfill their creative potential. As a licensed psychotherapist, career coach, human resources consultant, and writer, Gail has a wealth of knowledge and insight to share with her clients.

Gail has a B.A. from Connecticut College, an M.S.W. from Boston University, and a certificate in Human Resources from Bentley College. She has been published in the *National Business Employment Weekly, Nevada Woman,* and *Training,* and authored a collection of articles called *Success Strategies* for the Gonyea Career Center on America Online. She also wrote the highly acclaimed audiocassette workshop *Positive Choices: From Stress to Serenity,* featured in *The Improper Bostonian* and *Human Resource Executive.* To order *Positive Choices,* you can e-mail her at Prosuccess@aol.com with your Visa or Mastercard information, including the expiration date; fax her at 617-323-1963; or send a check for $16.95 to Gail McMeekin, Creative Success, 10 Langley Road, Suite 401, Newton Centre, MA 02459.

For further information about coaching, creativity workshops, or this book, including the women profiled, Gail can be reached at (617) 323-1442, by e-mail at Prosuccess@aol.com, or through her Web site: **www.creativesuccess.com.**